SO-AJP-290

LANCE ARMSTRONG

Images of a Champion

RODALE

© 2005 by Lance Armstrong and Graham Watson

Foreword © 2004 by Robin Williams

All rights reserved. No part of this publication may be reproduced or transmitted in any form or by any means, electronic or mechanical, including photocopying, recording, or any other information storage and retrieval system, without the written permission of the publisher.

Printed in Spain
Rodale Inc. makes every effort to use acid-free ∞, recycled paper ♻.

Linda Armstrong Kelly tribute from *No Mountain High Enough, Raising Lance, Raising Me* by Linda Armstrong Kelly with Joni Rodgers © 2005, Broadway, reprinted with permission.

Photographs by Graham Watson
Book design by Susan P. Eugster

Library of Congress Cataloging-in-Publication Data appeared in an earlier edition as:

Armstrong, Lance.
    Lance Armstrong : images of a champion / by Lance Armstrong ; photography
by Graham Watson; foreword by Robin Williams.
        p.   cm.
    ISBN 1-57954-891-1 hardcover
    1. Armstrong, Lance.   2. Armstrong, Lance–Pictorial works.   3. Bicycle racing–Pictorial
works.   I. Watson, Graham.   II. Title.
    GV1050.A76A77   2004
    796.6'2'092–dc22   2004041768

    ISBN-13 978-1-59486-246-5 paperback
    ISBN-10 1-59486-246-X paperback

Distributed to the book trade by Holtzbrinck Publishers

2   4   6   8   10   9   7   5   3   1   paperback

RODALE
LIVE YOUR WHOLE LIFE™

We inspire and enable people to improve their lives and the world around them
For more of our products visit **rodalestore.com** or call 800-848-4735

DEDICATION

FOR OCH

Thanks for giving me my start

and so much more.

—LANCE ARMSTRONG

★

CONTENTS

◀ Lance flying with
Bill Stapleton to the
Bristol-Myers Squibb
Tour of Hope,
St. Louis, Missouri,
October 2003.

FOREWORD

The Tour de France means many things to countless people. It is part Mardi Gras/Rose Bowl Parade with the promotional caravans, women in costumes strapped to the floats, smiling and throwing swag to the crowds at 60 miles an hour. It is part Nascar without the explosions, with multi-bicycle crashes where the *merde* hits the fan. But for me, as for many others over the last 6 years, the Tour de France has meant one thing: Lance Armstrong.

I believe it was very disconcerting for the French to have had their national sports event usurped by the man affectionately dubbed The Uni-baller. After each of his wins the Hotel de Crillon flies the Texas flag, looking like the Alamo de-signed by Louis the XIV. At first I think they thought it was a scam; the chemotherapy was an elaborate ruse to mask some performance-enhancing drug. "It's only chemo, my little snail snackers." They held his urine and blood for a year, like a vintage Chardonnay that needed to be sam-pled by candlelight at a great restaurant. I joked that they complained, "He has one testicle, he is more aerodynamic."

It took them until the tour of 2003 to appreciate him; when he showed his *humanité*. During the first individual time trial, he lost 12 pounds of water, looking like Lawrence of Arabia after coming through the Sahara, with salt-caked lips, to finish second. He was in a group crash. He got back up. He went off-road through a minefield of broken glass and condoms to avoid another crash. The *coup de grace* was the crash on the Luz-Ardiden, snagged by a child with a *musette* (who I believe was a midget in a wig). Lance got back up, and then almost fell again on a bike that would barely hold together. With anger, adrenaline, and his enormous reserve of talent, he won the stage. He had overcome the odds. He was no longer invin-cible, no longer a super-being. He showed he was human, and so the French finally embraced him. He had made mistakes and yet he was the same Lance, honestly acknowledging that without his teammates he could not have won.

It is a heavy burden, the mantle of "hero." He is this to many—for conquering his battle with cancer, as much as for winning on the mountains of the French countryside. He carries this weight with all of the grace and talent and motivation pos-sible—he takes nothing for granted. That is why for 5 years, I have been a member of the *Maillot Jaune* Posse, a camp follower of the "Blue Train of the Postal Jerseys," and why I am the *comique domes-tique* for my dawg and the *Equipe Postale.* For this reason, I raise my glass of fake beer and say, *"Vive La France"* and *"Vive Le Lance."*

—ROBIN WILLIAMS

◀ Lance and Robin Williams at a Tour stage-start in Bordeaux, 2003

★

INTRODUCTION

"Hi, I'm Lance." The outstretched hand came across in greeting, and I looked to where those three short words had come from, eyeing a young man with a dark swirl of hair across his forehead, a warm smile spread across his face, and a set of brightly intense eyes that seemed to be carrying a message to me, as yet undefined. His handshake was much stronger than I'd expected from a complete stranger but then this was no ordinary stranger. Motorola's PR man, Paul Sherwen, had warned me to look out for the Texan at the team's training camp in Santa Rosa, California, where I was shooting the team's publicity postcards and media guide in mid-January 1992. It seemed that this polite youngster had been a promising triathlete and had an even more promising career ahead of him as part of Motorola's long-term commitment to pro cycling in the USA and around the world. "Be warned," Sherwen said. "He's a bit special."

After that brief encounter, I quickly forgot all about him until 2 days later when all 16 guys on the team lined up on a quiet back road for their individual action shots. It was Armstrong who insisted on having his picture taken first—a rather bold attitude from someone who would not actually become a pro until 7 months later, after the Barcelona Olympics, and who had legendary cyclists like Andy Hampsten, Phil Anderson, and Steve Bauer as his peers on this exciting team. Surprised that none of these hard men even raised an eyebrow, I set to work on the rookie, instructing him to sprint along in the slipstream of the motor-

bike on a small hill amongst the Sonoma wine plantations. No sooner had I run off the first few frames than I realized this was, indeed, no ordinary cyclist. He exuded a confidence far beyond his years and had a steely aura that hinted of great things to come. Even then, he knew exactly how he wanted to look on camera and seemed to relish this small part of his baptism into pro cycling. I was immediately taken by him, impressed and motivated to take many more shots than was actually needed for such a simple task. I could tell how special he was by the way he stared right at me through the lens.

More than 10 years since that first encounter in 1992, Lance Armstrong is still filling my viewfinder with memorable images. I've been privileged and so fortunate to capture him winning an abundance of races around the world—World Championships, one-day classics, Tour de France stages, Olympic medals. You name it. Lance has won it. That meeting way back in time holds far more significance to me than if I'd bumped into Armstrong in the middle of the 1999 Tour de France. I realize now that his eyes back in 1992 had been telling me one thing in particular: We were going to be seeing a lot of each other over the years. We've both made enormous progress, too. Now, all of these years later, if I'm shooting the U.S. Postal Team's publicity pictures, Lance doesn't insist on having his pictures taken first, he merely asks.

Just in case anyone reading this book is neither a

cyclist, cycling fan, or Armstrong admirer, it has to be stated that Lance Armstrong has the enviable capacity to change peoples' lives or at least to influence or enrich their day-to-day existence. I am no different than those people, despite the fact that I've been rubbing shoulders with cycling stars like Lance for over 20 years. Whether I'm photographing him during a mountain stage of the Tour de France, in the intimacy of one of his spacious homes, or aboard a private Gulfstream jet as he commutes between cancer-awareness functions, the message is the same—Armstrong is one very special person. To spend just one minute in the man's company leaves you feeling like you're on cloud nine, to spend any longer with him is tantamount to changing your entire life. Well, if he hasn't actually managed that, he has at the very least enhanced my life considerably.

It was only through Lance that I began to understand some of the pressures of trying to win a Tour de France in a behind-the-scenes assignment at the 2000 Tour. It was through Lance that I was given glimpses of his life as a true celebrity, whether as the principal in a Nike commercial shoot or as the recipient of a six-car police escort diverting other vehicles so that Lance Armstrong, cancer survivor and sports legend, can make it to a second charity function. Most importantly, it was through Lance that I learned the little I do know of the fight against cancer. For it is there, away from the clamor of his sport's fans that another, more real Lance Armstrong emerges as an ambassador for the world of the cruel illness that almost took his life some years ago.

This book is an attempt to illustrate Lance's fight to be the best in the world, twice over. For sure, Lance was one of the best cyclists in the world when cancer crept up on him in 1996, but it is the story of the second part of his young life that has created the genuine hero the world now loves and reveres. Back in late 1996, I was faced with the decision of whether or not to incarcerate my entire collection of Armstrong images to an archive reserved solely for retired cyclists. For no one knew if Lance would ever race again, that is if he actually lived. But he is still living and with a hundred times more passion, commitment, and determination to succeed, to survive, than ever before. Yet this is not a book about cancer, nor is it just a book about a talented bike rider. It is quite simply a book that contains images of a champion, of one of the world's most special people, Lance Armstrong.

For sure Lance Armstrong's presence in the sport of cycling has thrilled millions of people. So powerful is the man's influence over the sport that, as long as Lance continues to race a bicycle for a living, any race without his presence is a race almost not worth photographing at all.

—GRAHAM WATSON

◀ Lance Armstrong poses for his team postcard in Santa Rosa, California, in 1992.

CHAPTER ONE

1992: EARLY DAYS

★ This is the year I made my debut into the European-based world of professional cycling. Although I wouldn't get a professional license for another 6 months, I was already wearing Motorola colors in January and becoming acquainted with my future teammates, Phil Anderson, Andy Hampsten, and Steve Bauer at the team's preseason training camp in northern California. The camp was fun. We mixed long, steady group rides with media training and even some wine tasting around the hills of Sonoma. I was really impressed with Anderson and Bauer—two men who had both worn the Yellow Jersey of the Tour de France and who were amongst the top one-day classics riders of that era. It was these two and, of course, Sean Yates, who guided me toward my first professional races after the Barcelona Olympics that August.

I'd raced in Europe before as a member of amateur national U.S. squads and was really excited about the prospects of racing against the big boys now. Of course, I wanted to start my pro career as the newly crowned Olympic road champion and had, therefore, made that race in Barcelona the major target of my season. As it turned out, the race was disappointing because I'd gone there thinking I could win and would win. But even though I attacked and tried to start or join in the right moves, in the end I missed the three-man escape that decided the race. A few years later, Fabio Casartelli, the Olympic winner from Italy, would join the Motorola Team and leave an indelible mark on my life that I could never have imagined possible.

I was surrounded by good people with good advice at Motorola, but none of it helped very much when I came in last at the Clasica San Sebastian in Spain. Pro cyclists race differently than amateurs, so I became a victim of their sudden accelerations that started about 60 kilometers before the end of this 240-kilometer classic. Dropped well before the last climbs, I wanted to stop the race and go home, but Hennie Kuiper, Motorola's assistant *directeur sportif,* talked me out of it, telling me how important it was to finish this first big race. I reluctantly continued all the way into San Sebastian, embarrassed and demoralized to be crossing the line so very long after the winner, Raul Alcala.

But Kuiper's advice had been good for me, and I vowed to myself that things would be different. I won a stage of the Vuelta a Galicia a few days later and then went to Zurich for the next big World Cup race and came in second. The difference between last place in San Sebastian and second in Zurich was purely a state of mind. I'd gone into the Swiss race believing the course wasn't as hard as people said, that the entire opposition was no better than me, and that therefore I had a chance to win. As it turned out, a great Russian cyclist was more clever than me—Viatcheslav Ekimov. Still, second place gave me some satisfaction and I looked forward to the remainder of the season, safe in the knowledge that I'd soon learn how to handle myself in big races and that I'd made at least some small impression on my peers.

◀ Training with Andy Hampsten, Christophe Manin, and Phil Anderson in northern California's wine country

1

△ 1992 Olympic Champion, Fabio Casartelli

◀ In a mid-race break with Davide Rebellin in Barcelona

▶ Cornering alongside Scott Sunderland and Allan Peiper in the final stage of the 1992 Nissan International Classic in Ireland. The crowds there were immense. Most of them were cheering for Sean Kelly, but they motivated all of us.

CHAPTER TWO

1993: FIRST SUCCESSES

★ I couldn't wait for the 1993 season to begin. I'd trained hard all winter, anticipating my first-ever Spring Classics, Tour de France, and then trying to win the World Championships. The Classics were real eye-openers, and, in hindsight, I realized that I was out of my depth in some of them. You can train hard, plan hard, and even race hard. But nothing prepares you for the cut-and-thrust nature of racing events like the Het Volk, Ronde Van Vlaanderen, and Ghent–Wevelgem and the brutal, bone-shaking experiences that come with each of them. I soon realized that I had an awful lot to learn but still managed to enjoy these exciting races. I also rode the hilly classics like Fleche Wallonne and Liège–Bastogne–Liège and felt that perhaps I had more chance in these events.

By the end of April, the Tour was on the horizon, but it took me weeks to finally persuade Jim Ochowicz that I could actually ride the Tour at the age of 21. Och finally relented, but with the strict understanding that I was to stop at the halfway mark. Still, it meant I could target some of the stages before the Alps, especially the stage to Verdun, which had a nasty climb about 10 kilometers from the end. As it turned out, my dream came perfectly true and I managed to escape over the hill with half a dozen others, and then outsprint them all at the finish. I was ecstatic. I'd won my first Tour stage in my first Tour de France! That day we had a four-star U.S. general in the team car. He came with about five armed guards! I'd really given him something to tell his troops back at NATO headquarters in Brussels. Four days later, my Tour was over. As planned, I quit after finishing the stage to Isola 2000. But my eyes had been opened to the beauty and attraction of the Tour. I wanted to come back to it as soon as possible. We were made for each other.

If the Tour was great, the World Championships in Oslo, Norway, were to be even greater. I'd kept myself out of trouble all day, avoiding the many crashes on this center-city circuit. With a few laps remaining, I was comfortably part of a 35-man lead group that had come together after almost 6 hours of racing. In the last lap, I made a big attack on the long hill north of the city, expecting and hoping it would draw away some others to form the winning move. Nobody took up the challenge, though, and I pedaled away by myself, not daring to think I'd make it all the way to the finish. With 10 kilometers to go, I was still out in front, still wondering why no one was coming after me.

Then I received word that Miguel Indurain was in fact chasing hard behind me. So I pedaled even faster! I couldn't have pressed harder on the pedals if I'd been Superman himself. I will remember the long road to the finish for as long as I live. It was packed with thousands of cheering people. It was a moment to cherish when the finish line came up on me and I became the youngest-ever Professional World Cycling Champion. Eventually I found Och and my mom. We danced and hugged each other in the road. What a great year it had been for me. It would be tough to beat this in 1994.

◄ Milan-San Remo is a long race–300 kilometers–so British Champ Sean Yates and I had to amuse ourselves at least part of the way. Sean was fast becoming my "main man" at Motorola. I could spend hours upon hours listening to his tactical experiences told across the dinner table or while we were sharing hotel rooms or just riding along.

▲ I'm getting close-up advice from Jim Ochowicz in the season-opening classic, the Omloop Het Volk, where the temperature rarely rises above 36°F (2°C) and where the Belgians seem to race as if this was their own private world championship.

◄ Here, I'm climbing ahead of Andre Tchmil on the Kemmelberg in the Ghent-Wevelgem Classic, a cobbled monster. This hill is best ridden only when it's dry. The descent is a nightmare. There are always loads of bad crashes.

▲ Champagne! Phil Anderson and I prepare to celebrate the Verdun victory. Manager Och was a great believer
in the tradition that all victories deserve toasting with copious quantities of alcohol—I wasn't complaining!

▶ We were celebrating going home. I'm joking with my soigneur Freddy Viane after the finish of the stage to Isola 2000.
This was a tough Alpine stage that saw me lose over 20 minutes by the end. Those were the early days!

◀ A sensational first-ever stage-win at Verdun in the 1993 Tour de France—definitely a career highlight.

▲ My two best friends—Mom and Och—were the first to congratulate me after the finish.

▶ I was the proudest man in the world when they played the U.S. national anthem.

◀ The historic victory at Oslo in 1993 at age 21. I had become
the youngest winner ever of a professional world road race championship.

▲ JT Neal was a great friend who I adored so much. I was still renting my apartment from him even
after I'd become world champion, and he'd always be looking after my affairs when I was away in Europe.
He was a great masseur, too! Sadly, JT died from cancer just after I won my fourth Tour de France in 2002.

◄ I used to borrow JT's speedboat to hang out with my friends on Lake Austin and to practice my other passion at that time—
water skiing. It was to take me a few more years before I could afford my own boat as well as a house on the lake shore.

▲ I used to be a collector of Ansel Adams photography and loved to shoot my own images whenever I could. This is inside my rented apartment, late 1993.

▶ Another beautiful sunset on Lake Travis in Austin, Texas.

CHAPTER THREE

1994: RAINBOW MAN

★ By the time I ventured back into European racing, it had been almost 7 months since I'd become World Champion, and my life had changed more than just a little bit. I'd become something of a media star since the previous August but had yet to appreciate the responsibilities of wearing the famed Rainbow Jersey of a World Champion. We had our first-ever European pre-season training camp in Tuscany, which itself followed a tough first race in the Ruta Mexico in January. I was in fairly good shape and really wanted to show myself in the Belgian one-day classics, but I'd become a thoroughly marked man in the flatter, cobbled races. Again, I seemed more capable in the Fleche Wallonne and Liège–Bastogne–Liège races, where natural strength would allow me to dictate the racing a little more than in Flanders. I used "the Fleche" as training for Liège and watched from afar as three Italians from the same team rode away from everyone else to take the first three places in Huy.

When one of those same three Italians—in fact, an Italian-based Russian, Evgeni Berzin—then won Liège–Bastogne–Liège by himself, it shocked me to realize how much I still needed to improve. I'd chased Berzin home, finishing in second place. But, I thought to myself, *One day I will win Liège!* Thirteenth place in the Amstel Gold signaled the end of my springtime campaign, and I headed home to the U.S., hoping to win the Tour DuPont for the first time. Only the strong and wily Ekimov beat me once again. The DuPont, at 12 days, was the longest stage race I'd ridden in my life, but I began to like the concept of stage racing more and more. It was so different from one-day racing, and each day was like a day in school—always learning something new.

I'd become slightly disillusioned after losing the DuPont race and had hoped to rectify things by winning a stage of the Tour. The Motorola Team had put an awful lot of energy and preparation into winning the team time trial between Calais and the Channel Tunnel terminals. We rode the course so many times over a period of 1 week, prior to the Tour, that we felt it was made for us—long, rolling climbs and wide-open, wind-swept descents—not a conventional time trial. But we ended in second place, a mere 6 seconds off the pace of Johan Museeuw's GB-MG Team. One week later, things were no better when Miguel Indurain caught me for a full 3 minutes in the stage nine time trial at Bergerac. That was bad enough, but then Big Mig took another 2 minutes out of me by the end of 64 kilometers! After that, I barely made it through the Pyrenees, because I was feeling so lousy about myself. All I could hope for was a return to form for the defense of my world title in Sicily, but in the end I just didn't have it on the day, finishing in seventh place after a manic last-lap battle. I ended my season in the Paris–Tours classic and went home to winter in Austin with the realization I had to do much better in 1995.

◄ First race of 1994 and first competitive outing as World Champion—the Ruta Mexico. This was a tough debut, considering how busy the winter had been and how far away the real European season was. The Motorola Team rode this race in January as a favor to teammate Raul Alcala, who wanted to impress his Mexican public and as a business gesture for Motorola, who was moving into Mexico big time.

▲ Steve Bauer was another mate at Motorola. I can't remember the joke, but it was obviously a good one!

◀ Raul Alcala and I were always good friends.

◀◀ Max Testa, our team doctor, picked up a new friend in Tuscany that January.

▶ Tirreno-Adriatico is a great warm-up race for Milan–San Remo, and the Italians love anyone wearing the Rainbow Jersey! But Paris–Nice is the better race by far, so 1994 was the first and last time I rode this "race between two seas."

◄ On the cobblestones of the Tour of Flanders in 1994, at this point, I was coming under pressure to perform well with the World Champion's jersey on my back. But Flanders is the toughest one-day race on the calendar, and I knew I was a marked man throughout the race.

▲ As World Champion, the media expects great things. This is me explaining my second place in the Liège–Bastogne–Liège classic of 1994.

▲ Sean Yates became race-leader in the 1994 Tour for the first time in his life. I insisted on being photographed with him, the two of us standing so proudly in our legendary jerseys—definitely one for the scrapbook!

▲ This is me chatting with Jean-Marie Leblanc alongside his organizer's car in the 1994 Tour. An English-speaking Jean-Marie seemed to appreciate an American presence in the sport.

▶ This is Motorola in full flight where I'm heading for second place in the Boulogne-sur-Mer team time trial in the 1994 Tour. I'm in third place, wearing white, with Phil Anderson and Sean Yates ahead of me. "Yatesy" is setting a brutal pace for us to follow, as he always does. We missed first place by just 6 seconds, beaten by Johan Museeuw's GB-MG Team.

JIM OCHOWICZ

FORMER MOTOROLA TEAM DIRECTOR

I first heard about Lance Armstrong from Wayne Stetina of Shimano. Wayne described a young triathlete who was a powerhouse on the bike and would make a great bike racer. I was skeptical as I had heard the same thing about a number of triathletes, but I kept the name in the back of my mind.

I first saw Lance race during the Richmond Criterium Stage of the 1991 Tour DuPont. Lance was in the break with Sean Yates. Lance didn't win but came in third behind Yates. I recalled his name and now had a face to put with the name.

I first met Lance during that same 1991 Tour DuPont. Chris Carmichael, the National Team coach, asked me if I wanted to meet Lance. I told Chris to have Lance give me a call. He called immediately and we planned to get together that very night. Within seconds of our meeting, I knew I liked him. He had a powerful presence and tremendous energy. We talked about everything, including racing in Europe and the Tour de France. By the end of that first conversation, I knew I had met someone special.

I got my chance to work with Lance later that year. I signed a 2-year renewal contract with Motorola. Now I had the opportunity to elevate the team and look to add some new talent. My first thought was to contact Lance. I arranged to meet him in Germany where he was racing and preparing for the World Championships.

◄ Whenever Lance called me up in the car, he would say one of two things, "What are you doing, Och?" or "Jimmy, me legs feel GREAT." The latter always meant a win, always!

In my experience, riders tend to be more open on their bikes than in an office. So, I brought my bike to Germany as well as the contract. I hoped to go on a few training rides with Lance and discuss some business during those rides. We were together for a few days before he finally agreed to the terms and signed the contract to race for the Motorola Cycling Team in 1992 and 1993. I had secured the team's future.

Lance's professional career began in 1992. His first race was the Clasica San Sebastian World Cup event. Despite Lance's eagerness, the race was a bit much for him (as it would have been for every new professional). He wanted to stop but Hennie Kuiper, *directeur sportif*, insisted he finish the race. Lance did cross the line, but in last place.

Lance was undaunted by his experience in San Sebastian and wanted another chance. He believed in himself, and his confidence was infectious. A week later, we brought him to the World Cup in Zurich where he showed glimpses of his real potential. He finished second to Viatcheslav Ekimov, who would later become a U.S. Postal teammate. At the highest level of racing, Lance went from last place to second place within 2 weeks. Unbelievable!

Lance started the 1993 season with lofty goals for such a young racer. He wanted to race the Spring Classics, Tour de France, and World Road Cycling Championships. These goals are beyond the reach of your average second-year professional. Lance was never "average."

He started the 1993 season with a win at the Trophee Laigueglia, beating Moreno Argentin in the final kilometers. He then won the U.S. Pro Road Championship. Lance, of course, wanted to ride in the Tour de France. We agreed to take him but only if he agreed to pull out when we decided the time was right. He won the stage into Verdun, becoming the youngest rider in history to win a stage in the Tour de France. He finished off the season with a win at the World Championships in Oslo, Norway.

Lance is a born leader. He possesses passion, intelligence, intensity, focus, and amazing dedication and drive. His work ethic is simply unparalleled. These qualities are infectious. He inspires those around him to rise above and exceed any expectations.

The 2004 Tour de France was something really special. Unlike the 1999 miracle ride, this was the culmination of all five Tour de France victories. It had the feel of a magical performance of epic proportions, watching the team and Lance deliver day after day, a flawless show of strength, strategy and emotion wrapped into every pedal stroke. Never did anyone fail to deliver or impress.

The clincher for me was the team time trial. Under some of the worst conditions a racing cyclist could face, not to mention the inherent danger surrounding this event itself, the U.S. Postal Team succeeded in winning the event, putting in motion their dominance of the 2004 Tour.

We have all come to expect the unbelievable from Lance. Once again, he has delivered the goods, making history in the process. Thank you, Lance!

▲ Paris-Nice was one of the races meant to push me toward race-
winning form in 1995. Here I am going for it on a stage to Le Grand Duc,
but the form was still missing, and I was overtaken
by the eventual winner, Pascal Richard.

▶ The 1995 Milan-San Remo started right next to the impressive
Il Duomo in the center of Milan. It is an awesome setting
for the start of a great classic.

CHAPTER FOUR

1 9 9 5 : A T R A G I C T O U R

★ People always said I was impetuous when I first began racing as a pro. In hindsight, it was probably true. This is okay if you are winning a lot, but I wasn't! The result being that I had to keep overcoming disappointing results and getting my head together in time for the next race—a difficult thing to do when the results just don't go your way. I'd trained more than ever before in the winter and again rode in all the one-day classics of northern Europe, except Paris–Roubaix, which I've yet to ride even to this day! Once again, Liège–Bastogne–Liège was my best performance of the Spring Classics—sixth place behind winner Mauro Gianetti. But apart from that and a stage win in the Paris–Nice race, I had little or nothing to show for my winter's dedication. More and more, my mind was turning to the challenge of stage racing, and it was partly this new prospect that pushed me to win the 1995 Tour DuPont where I beat Viatcheslav Ekimov this time, and by a full 2 minutes.

I'd won a time trial, a flat stage, and a stage that finished up at Beech Mountain in the Appalachian Mountains of North Carolina. This wasn't the Tour de France, but I'd raced well and hard over 11 stages and felt I'd turned some psychological corner in my mind. Maybe stage racing was where my forté really lay. With the DuPont success buoying me, I viewed the real Tour with fresh eyes and mind and couldn't wait to see what I could do. Then tragedy struck. On only the second day in the Pyrenees, there was a big crash on the descent of the Col de Portet d'Aspet and a teammate of ours lay dead in the road. Fabio Casartelli had only joined the team that winter, but we'd quickly come to accept and like him enormously. His presence in the Tour spoke volumes for the talent he had, a talent that would never be fulfilled. His death was a devastating blow to everyone on the Tour, not just Motorola, but it came down to us to decide that the race should go on, albeit a neutralized stage the next day.

Two days before, I'd almost won a stage after a tough breakaway with a Russian, Sergei Outschakov, but stupidly waited for the sprint, thinking I was the better sprinter. On the neutralized stage to Pau, I became more motivated than I could ever remember and vowed to win a stage of this tragic Tour for Fabio. My chance came 2 days later, and I attacked about 20 kilometers from Limoges, riding on pure adrenalin with the peloton apparently strung out in pursuit behind me. It was a relief to finally win another Tour stage, but more than that it was a fitting way to pay homage to Fabio. I was still thinking of him a few weeks later, after I'd won the Clasica San Sebastian and went to sleep that night marveling at the power human beings have to overcome such grief and use it to better their own lives. I knew I'd learned a lot about life from just that Tour and hoped I'd become a better person—and cyclist—for it. At least I'd managed to finish the Tour for the first time in my life.

◀ Tragedy struck on the Tour de France when our teammate, Fabio Casartelli, died after a bad crash on stage fifteen. The next day we rode a ceremonial stage into Pau. The rest of the peloton eased up in the last kilometer to allow us our lonely, symbolic freedom as we crossed the line alone.

▲ At Tarbes on July 19, I stand bewildered and distraught during a minute's silence to our late, great teammate, Fabio Casartelli. As race-leader, Miguel Indurain (left) joined us at the front of the peloton.

▲ I couldn't ride with anyone as the race pulled away from the start on a ceremonial stage to Pau. I just wanted to be alone with my thoughts, reflecting on the life of a wonderful, friendly teammate and companion.

It took me a few days to achieve, but I stormed into Limoges on stage eighteen, alone, so happy to win a Tour stage and give Casartelli the greatest tribute that myself and my team could offer him in memoriam. The pointed fingers were my only means to truly communicate my feelings to Fabio.

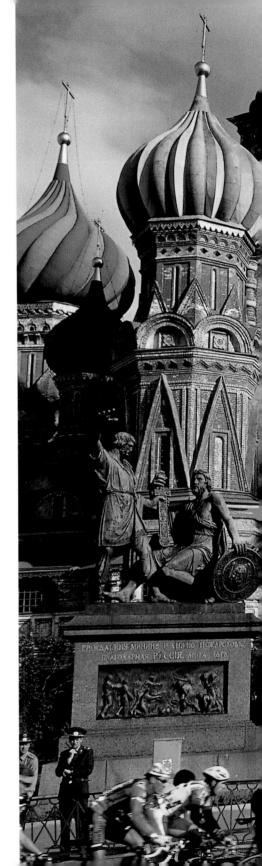

◄ Motorola, under the impetus of Och, created a trust fund
for Casartelli's only child as well as a superb marble monument close
to the point where Casartelli met his death on the Col du Portet d'Aspet.
In late November, the principals of the team posed respectfully in front
of the newly opened memorial. I'm between Noel DeJonckheere (far left),
Max Testa, Jim Ochowicz, Hennie Kuiper, and Paul Sherwen.

▲ Happy days! Three years after coming home last in the Clasica
San Sebastian, I've won the 1995 edition by myself and laid to rest
more than a few ghosts.

▶ The Tour de France stars rode in Moscow, just one week after the
end of the French race, in a one-off invitational event for charity.
We seem to be dwarfed by the might of St Basil's Cathedral in Red Square.

CHAPTER FIVE

1996: TRIUMPH THEN TEARS

★ Another solid winter of training preceded what I hoped would be my best-ever season in 1996. Now I was certain my future lay in multi-day races in which a mistake or misfortune on one day could be rectified on another, in some cases. The season's plans still included the one-day classics, but with more impetus on the hillier ones than those held on the cobbled roads of Flanders. I'd had a good Paris–Nice, finishing second overall, and then set my sights on the Fleche Wallonne, winning it in handsome style after dropping my breakaway companions on the steep, wall-like climb to the finish. Part two of the Motorola plan was to also win Liège–Bastogne–Liège 4 days later. But I made a mess of the finish, gifting the race to Switzerland's Pascal Richard in the sprint, after we'd forged a long breakaway in company with Mauro Gianetti over the last 35 kilometers. Yes, I was still learning.

Somewhere between that Liège debacle and winning a second Tour DuPont a few weeks later, I noticed my strength fluctuating a lot. One day I'd be super-strong, the next as weak as a kitten. The pattern continued well after the DuPont race, where I'd taken another three stages and felt more and more like a Tour rider. If only I could get my weight down without losing strength, I felt I had enough years ahead of me to challenge for a decent overall place in the Tour. But the 1996 Tour was a very rapid affair for me—less than six stages, in fact—for I abandoned early in the rain-drenched stage to Aix-les-Bains, not knowing why or understanding what was wrong with me. But something was wrong, that I knew for sure. I'd had trouble breathing normally for a few days now. Thus it was that the main target of the season, the Atlanta Olympic Games, came and went with miserable consequences. Sixth place in the time trial was my best performance.

I then set my sights on the World Championships in October, believing I'd find the form just as I had in 1993. I headed back to Europe after the Olympics to race in the Clasica San Sebastian and Grande Prix Suisse (formerly the Championship of Zurich). But whatever had been wrong with me in early May was still with me now in late August. So I quit the season after the Swiss race to go home and get some rest. I was sure that was all I needed—rest. The world now knows just how much rest I got after I was diagnosed with testicular cancer on October 2, 1996, and I found out just how totally unimportant my career as a professional cyclist really was. At least that's how I felt when facing death in the eye as a 25-year-old man normally so very full of energy and ambition. So as Johan Museeuw became World Champion in Lugano that October, I was a million miles away, praying for a miracle that would save my life.

◄ Paris–Nice—and, therefore, Laurent Jalabert—was my first big target of 1996. I tried so hard to beat the Frenchman (we dueled on at least three of the stages) but in the end he was the strongest, and I ended in second place overall. If nothing else, I was pleased with my climbing, which had improved, and the Spring Classics were just around the corner.

▶ Victory in the Fleche Wallonne—next to my World Championship victory of 1993, this was my biggest win, and I savored the moment as I approached the finish line on the Mur de Huy.

▲ Yes, I was pleased with my win in Fleche Wallone, but I now wanted the double victory in next Sunday's Liège-Bastogne-Liège to accomplish a feat achieved by only a rare few such as Eddy Merckx and Bernard Hinault.

◀ Believing I was the strongest sprinter in the final escape, I waited until the finish to make my big effort. But Pascal Richard was faster, or more clever, and I made second. It was a stupid mistake, as I could have probably dropped Richard on the final climb.

▲ I'm not too happy with things in Liège, as this image shows.

▶ Beech Mountain was, as always, the decisive climb in the race. Here I am giving it my all with 6 kilometers to go, heading for stage and overall victory with just the time trial to come. It was at this point that I knew my climbing was improving enormously, and a future as a Tour contender was not out of the question either.

▶▶ The Tour DuPont helped make amends somewhat for Liège. I was determined to score a second victory in this event in 1996 and had assembled the very best team Motorola had to offer. The best teammate in the mountains was unquestionably Axel Merckx, who rode at my side throughout the race.

▲ The Tour DuPont brought Tour de France-style racing to the U.S. in a way not seen since the days of the Coors Classic. It did fantastic things for American cycling and is badly missed even now, 8 years after its demise.

▲ Winning a DuPont stage into Greensboro, I was in the best form of my life and could hardly wait to get back to Europe to race the Tour and see what I could achieve in the high mountains.

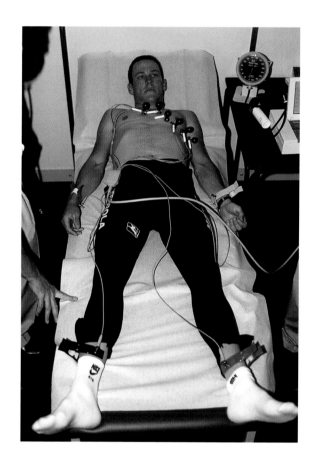

▲ All Tour riders have to undergo a largely superficial medical test the day before the Tour prologue. As I lay there in Heertogenbosch, The Netherlands, July 1996, I had no idea of the true nature of my physical health.

▲ I stopped after just 35 kilometers of stage six, humiliated yet incapable of riding any further. Hennie Kuiper, Motorola's assistant team director, offered encouragement and sympathy, but I felt like a quitter all the same.

◄ The Olympic Games saw me hungry for a gold medal, and I started the race in exuberant form, hoping
to control things until the final move came. Here I am climbing the main hill ahead of all my rivals—Bjarne Riis,
Abraham Olano, Laurent Jalabert, and Andrei Tchmil, with teammate George Hincapie lurking back there in case I messed up.

▲ Still determined to make the Worlds my main target of the year, I rode in the Clasica San Sebastian one week after the Olympics.
Here, I'm chatting with Jan Ullrich, star and runner-up of the 1996 Tour, and a man for whom I had an awful lot of respect.
Jan had become amateur World Champion 24 hours before me in 1993—I was happy for his success in the 1996 Tour,
but I had no inkling that we'd become such great rivals a few years later. As it was, San Sebastian was one of my last races before
I abandoned the season with health problems. It would be more than a year before I made my return to European racing.

MIGUEL INDURAIN
5-TIME WINNER OF THE TOUR DE FRANCE

Who could have told me that this racer with such talent and such strength, although he was not a great climber, would one day win the Tour de France? Who could have told me that, moreover, he would not just win one Tour, but five, and then six?

From the first races in which I competed with him, I remember his acceleration breaking away from the pack, which was powerful, but if there is one thing I remember it is the World Championship in which he beat me in Oslo, in September 1993. There we were, a group of racers who had escaped forward from the pack, but there was no agreement among us, and, approaching the finish line, the least known of us was the one to attack. It was Lance Armstrong, with whom we could not catch up. From then on, his list of achievements began to grow, although he had already won one leg of the Tour earlier that year.

From the very beginning, people said that he was a young man with a lot of talent, and he was demonstrating it, although at no time after seeing him in action did I think that he could manage to win the Tour de France. He was inconsistent, perhaps due to his youth, and his forte were the cycling classics and stages. In 1994, thanks to the Rainbow Jersey, he made an important place for himself in the pack, although as luck would have it he was not a direct rival of mine because he did not compete in the general classification.

The following year, in 1995, he won another leg in the Tour (Limoges), which he dedicated to Fabio

◀ Miguel Indurain is shown here in action at Luz-Ardiden in the 1994 Tour.

Casartelli, the racer from Motorola, a teammate of his who had died in a descent in the Pyrenees. Lance's fine physical conditioning continued to be evident, although he remained out of the general classification of the Tour.

It was in 1996, my last year as an active racer, when the pack learned that he was suffering testicular cancer. I don't remember exactly how I found out, but I suppose that it was through the newspapers, since his illness became officially known on the occasion of the World Competition in Lugano (Switzerland), and I didn't compete in that race. Earlier, in August, I had been with him in the United States, where we saw each other in the Olympic Games in Atlanta. Like the American that he is, he wanted to win, but couldn't. As he himself later acknowledged, he was already ill, although he didn't know it at the time.

I left cycling that year and Lance left the pack to fight and beat cancer, which he fortunately accomplished. When he came back, he was a new cyclist, with fewer pounds and less body fat but the same qualities. So, in 1999 he won his first Tour when nobody, at least not I, thought that he could. During that winter his friend and previous coach of the Motorola Team, Jim Ochowicz, who was a member of the same commission that I was in the International Cycling Union, told me that Lance wanted me to attend the "Ride of the Roses" that he organizes each year in Austin, Texas, for the purpose of raising funds for his cancer foundation. I liked the idea and, in April 2000, I accepted the invitation and travelled to Austin with my family.

Lance was so busy that I barely had the chance to spend much time with him, but I was in his house, met his wife, and found out firsthand about the great work that they do on behalf of children and against cancer by way of the Lance Armstrong Foundation®. Honestly, although he had already won one Tour, I didn't think that he was going to have the great run that he has had, but it is clear that he has taken a liking to the Tour and knows the trick to it, that he knows how to prepare himself, and that it's his race.

I don't have a problem with his besting my record, because after beating cancer, what he has done is very commendable and, moreover, records are made to be broken. As if that weren't enough, I am of the opinion that all of us who cycle on this level are champions.

The fact is that Armstrong has now won six Tours, and it wouldn't be odd, seeing how easily he won the last one, to see him win once again in 2005. But the years always take a toll and some day his time will come too, it's a fact of life. So let us hope he takes heed of this and plans a last Tour campaign very carefully. Is he the best racer in the history of the Tour? Yes, why not, although Merckx and Hinault have won more in terms of yellow jerseys and stages. The fact is it is the fans, the aficionados, who decide the ultimate Tour champion even if they let themselves be guided sometimes by personal feelings rather than merits. We are talking about winning a Tour de France as if it were easy, when it is so difficult that very few people, in 100 years of history, have ever achieved it.

CHAPTER SIX

1998: BACK TO WORK

★ A miracle had happened, and I resolved to come back to the sport that I'd left in late 1996 to see if I could once again be a man to win classics, tours, and world championships. I wanted to simply be the best, to see just how high I could climb, and to maybe claw back the season-and-a-half I'd lost through illness. My coach, Chris Carmichael, had become fascinated with the huge weight loss from chemotherapy and had eagerly planned a training and racing program that could now build in the much improved weight-strength ratio. I was lighter and had, so he told me, the potential to climb long mountains at high speeds, and to climb with the sport's greatest climbers, if I trained right. First on the agenda was the Ruta del Sol, a 5-day stage race in southern Spain, followed by Paris–Nice, an old favorite of mine.

The Spanish race was fine; 5 days of solid training under warm sunshine. But the French race was a different matter, and I quit during the very first road stage, convinced that I didn't want to do this anymore. I'd tried to win the uphill prologue in Paris—but had only managed 23rd place. And then when the first stage began under the threat of snow, but offered merely freezing rain instead, I exited from the sport for the very last time, or so I thought. But no, I had better friends than I perhaps realized at the time. They came from all around me—Carmichael, Och, Bart Knaggs, John Korioth, Eddy Merckx, as well as some of my old teammates at Motorola, George Hincapie, Frankie Andreu, and Kevin Livingston—encouraging me to give it one more go, to not give in at the first sign of difficulty. It was Carmichael, Och, and ex-pro Bob Roll, who took me into the Appalachian Mountains to train harder and reinvent myself.

In June, over 3 months after quitting the sport, I came back to the Tour of Luxembourg—a tough little race—where we had competition in the form of Belgian, French, and Italian teams training for the Giro and Tour. I won the race overall, having won the very first stage in a sprint and then taken the Yellow Jersey on the very last stage when Andreu and myself broke away together. Andreu won that stage alone, to make it a great day for the U.S. Postal Team. Things were looking up! More weeks of training followed. Could I possibly make a serious attempt at winning the Worlds that October? Three weeks in the Vuelta a España proved I was going in the right direction. I had done well in time trials, my climbing had improved tenfold compared with pre-1996 levels, and all in all I felt ready for Valkenburg, Holland, and fourteen climbs of the Cauberg hill.

On race day, it was wet, cold, and windy—exactly the conditions I used to revel in—and I was proudly wearing the USA jersey for the first time since the 1996 Olympics in Atlanta. I really wanted to do well. In fact, I did do well but not quite well enough, taking fourth place in a hotly contested road race over 258 kilometers of a constantly challenging course. I didn't quite have the extra strength and reserves that I needed when the last lap attacks began with nearly 6 hours of racing in my legs. But I'd had a taste of success again and knew my future was in professional cycling. Roll on 1999!

◀ That's me in the red top, nervously waiting to sign on for the 1998 Ruta del Sol, my first race back after surviving cancer.

◀ But life at the top is tough—as is getting there. Right now, I'm shattered after a hilly stage of the Ruta and wondering if I made the right choice to return to racing.

▲ Paris-Nice was the next race on my comeback trail, but the hilly prologue was a monster to overcome. I became disillusioned and went home to Nice the very next day, not even completing the opening road stage.

▲ The Vuelta a España was the next race on the trail.
A steady fourth-place overall gave me great hope, especially
as it was the first 3-week tour I'd finished in 3 years.

▶ Crashes are part and parcel of my sport, but I've been
extremely lucky in staying clear of trouble most of the time.
Here, I have been caught up in a small crash in Paris–Tours.

◀◀ **PREVIOUS SPREAD**
The Vuelta a España is a great race and acts as a superb preparation
for the World Championships. The weather in September
is nearly always great, and the scenery so spectacular
that there's little chance of getting bored.

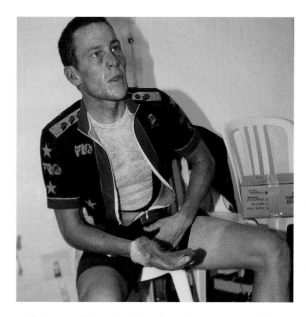

▲ Washing myself down after the road race, disappointment would
eventually give way to a realization that I hadn't done so badly.

▲ As always, Claudine Merckx was there to cheer me on at the start.
The Merckx family is almost my own I sometimes think! I used to love
staying with Eddy and his family in Brussels and spending long hours into
the night watching old videos and listening to Eddy tell tales of long ago.

◀ The Worlds in 1998 were my big target. But at the time, two fourth
places in both the time trial and road race were a bit disappointing,
to say the least. In the end, the cold, wet conditions conspired against me,
but at least I'd enjoyed myself.

JOHAN BRUYNEEL
USPS TEAM DIRECTOR

I can well remember racing against Lance in 1992, when I was one of the ONCE Team's top riders. People had said he was a big American talent, but he finished last in his first race, the Clasica San Sebastian. One week later, however, he'd won a stage of the Tour of Galicia where I'd been racing as well, then went on to the Championship of Zurich. That race was won by Viatcheslav Ekimov, and Lance finished second. So he showed already what a talent he was. My impressions of him from the start were that he had enormous potential, but that he had no experience at all. But he was to learn quickly! Lance and I always joke about a stage of the 1995 Tour to Liège in Belgium, which I was to win. I'd attacked on Mont Theux with Miguel Indurain and looked back to see Lance trying so hard to get across to us. But he never made it! Of course, he'd crashed a few days before and was covered in plasters, but it is still a special memory for me to now share with Lance. I'd dropped the man who would later win six Tours de France.

More than 3 years later, I had retired and was commentating for TV in the Tour of Spain where Lance was racing really well. By then I knew I was going to become the new *directeur* of the U.S. Postal Team for 1999, so it was even more interesting to see Lance tackle a big stage-race again. I remembered seeing him in the mountains in races like the Tour of Switzerland and Tour de France in 1995, and I thought, with specific training and a

◀ An unlikely scenario—ONCE star Johan Bruyneel paces rival Lance Armstrong in the 1995 Leeds Classic.

carefully prepared schedule, he could aim for a top ranking in the 1999 Tour. I said, "I think you have to focus on the Tour de France next year, I think you can win it." I can still see the crazy expression on his face, he probably thought: 'This guy is crazy.' But Lance never said, "No, that's not possible." For me, that was the first big step.

Over the winter of 1998, we planned a lot together, and I listened intently to hear what Lance himself wanted to achieve before structuring a plan that was remarkably similar to one I would have liked to have adopted if I'd been given the chance to choose my own direction as a rider. We started to work toward an ambitious goal…about which neither of us knew would work. When we started back in 1998, Lance was the perfect student. He accepted a new way of preparing the season and new objectives without asking what it was good for. He has continued to learn to the point where there's little left for me to teach him. And I, too, have learned a lot from Lance.

I've spent so many hours, days, weeks, and months in Lance's company that I probably know him as well as just about anyone else. He continues to amaze me, juggling an extremely hectic business life in the U.S. with the responsibilities that come from winning those five Tours de France. Yet I have never met a man more dedicated to the fulfilment of his profession as a cyclist. He is the most complete Tour rider of his generation, obsessed with training, reconnaissance, more training, and yet more reconnaissance. He never stops looking for

new ideas to strengthen his commitment to winning the Tour another time.

We have probably never been closer than in the 2003 Tour de France. We spent a lot of time in Lance's room after each stage, analyzing each situation as it developed. I always try to stay calm and show him that I have complete confidence in him. When the day didn't go well, I would say things like, "There's no way they can beat you, I'm sure that nobody has worked as hard as you. It has to pay off, sooner or later." It did, and it solidified an already strong relationship.

One of the greatest experiences during the last 6 years had to be stage fifteen to Luz-Ardiden of the 2003 Tour. Attacked by Ullrich on the Tourmalet, then the crash at the foot of the final climb, almost another crash because of a mechanical problem, and then to come back to the group to attack like he did—that was the Armstrong I had been waiting for the whole of the Tour. After his crash, I pulled up my car next to him to ask how he was. I didn't have the occasion to do that. He looked into my eyes with anger mixed with determination. When I saw that, I knew he was going to win the Tour again.

In my opinion, Lance was stronger in 2004 than in 1999. Having gone through a lot of situations with him in the past, I knew that he didn't want to give out any gifts. He wanted to win whenever he could. The first win was nice, but winning 6, especially considering the circumstances, was a nicer, sweeter feeling. Winning 6 tours in a row is something to be proud of. Lance is very proud and so am I.

CHAPTER SEVEN

1999: FIRST YELLOW

★ In 1999 we had the same team, but with a new manager, Johan Bruyneel. This season saw me back in Europe as early as the first day in February, craving to build on the relative successes of 1998 and to make a quantum leap in my resurrected career. It seems we were going to try and win the Tour de France. I was going to try to win the Tour de France! When Bruyneel suggested that to me at the previous year's Worlds, I thought he was mad, completely and utterly crazy, but I listened and the more I listened, the more I grew confident that it was perhaps doable. Bruyneel had a very successful racing career, with a third place overall in the Vuelta a España as his big tour highlight. The racing program he now suggested for me, I knew, he'd have wanted for himself if he'd been in a position to instigate it when he was still racing.

Chris Carmichael had it mapped out in scientific detail—when to train, where to train, when to race, where to race. But I would have to come to Le Puy de Fou on July 3 in the most perfect physical shape imaginable, and with my mind just right, too. Of course, no one gave me any great odds to win, not even after I'd won the 6.8-kilometer prologue on the same course used in the 1993 Tour prologue won by Miguel Indurain. And again, when I convincingly won the stage seven time trial at Metz, still no one was considering me as being the possible winner. But that's the way I preferred it because I was about to show my rivals and critics that Lance Armstrong was also a climber now. The mountainous stage to Sestriére went like clockwork, and I was able to attack with about 6 kilometers to go and win my first-ever mountain stage of a Tour de France.

The Alps came and went without any problems, as did the long haul south to the Pyrenees. I was enjoying my new role as leader of the Tour, enjoyed even more having at my disposal a team so loyal and dedicated that I hardly had to pedal all day it seemed. We enjoyed letting others win stages that year, letting the opportunists ride away all day to fight out the stage for themselves because we were so much in control and my position as *Maillot Jaune* (Yellow Jersey) so apparently impregnable. We made a lot of friends that year in the peloton, with the ONCE, Kelme, Telekom, and Lampre Teams gaining from our kind benevolence. After the Pyrenees had played their role in the Tour, my lead increased a little bit more and, well, it was as good as over. All that remained was the time trial at Futuroscope, another time gain over Alex Zulle, and then it was off to Paris with the Yellow Jersey on my back. I'd won the Tour de France—just as we'd planned it!

◀ This is the way it should be—Johan and I alone in the Pyrenees on one of our annual training rides to *reconnaître* the Tour route. This is definitely one of my favorite images. It says everything about what I do each spring when no one is around to observe.

◄ Several times each year I need to do an intensive hill-test to gauge my aerobic condition before the season really starts. There are a few quiet roads above Monaco where I always do the test. I hate it really, but it's a necessary part of my training routine, and it dictates how much more quality training I must do to be ready to race.

▲ I'd always try to ride to Monaco with my teammates, Kevin Livingston and Frankie Andreu. We'd always meet at the Nice war memorial on the Corniche, next to the Vieux Port of Nice, and Kevin would usually do the same test as me, except he was often faster than me!

◀ The first main race of 1999 was the Amstel Gold where I really tried hard to win
but ended up in a showdown with Holland's Michael Boogerd, who beat me by a tire width!

▲ I was not happy at all since this had been a major target of the year for me.
Yet a professional still has to respect the podium obligations. My face tells the real story!

▲ My first Yellow!

◄ Victory in the 1999 Tour prologue, a preview of things to come.

► The Passage du Gois on stage two of the 1999 Tour destroyed the hopes of many of my rivals, but we knew what to expect as we'd investigated the slippery nature of the sea-covered road a few days before the Tour had begun. That's why I am in that small group, along with George Hincapie, ahead of any trouble there may be. Thanks, Johan!

▶ In the crucial Metz time trial,
I was in my element, crucifying the opposition
to the point where I could afford to almost
cruise home on auto-pilot. I couldn't
resist giving Graham a friendly smile when
he got alongside me with 5 kilometers to go.

▲ All the same, it's hard riding at that speed. I welcomed the wet towel and
drink held out for me by masseuse Emma O'Reilly at the finish.

▶ My teammates George Hincapie and Kevin Livingston did me proud on stage nine
to Sestriére, constantly riding tempo at the front even on the toughest climbs. It was inspiring
stuff and made my ultimate task that much easier.

◄ I'm now on the Col du Galibier and feeling very, very good. Richard Virenque, Laurent Dufaux, and Alex Zulle are just about able to stay in contact.

▲ But I've attacked on the climb to Sestriére and I'm alone at last. It's a wonderful feeling being in Yellow, out in front, and in the Alps!

► A sweet victory—the Sestriére mountain has been conquered and I am a very happy stage-winner for the third time in this Tour. All those long, hard training rides finally paid off for me, and I felt on top of the world.

▲ In winning the time trial at Futuroscope, I'd achieved the satisfaction of winning all three of the Tour's stages against the clock, which is something only champions like Merckx, Hinault, and Indurain had done in their best years. It would have been so easy to lose my concentration with overall victory virtually assured. I rate this stage win as one of my best ever in a Tour de France. It was great to hear that Tyler Hamilton had taken third place in the stage—he'd worked so hard for me.

▲ Kristin and Mom jumped across to the podium for a special pose with me.

◀ I look serious in this shot, and with good reason—
the U.S. national anthem is blaring out across the Champs Elysees.
I'm the proudest man in the world, winner of my first ever Tour de France!

◄ One big happy family—I managed to get all my friends, relatives, and even neighbors into this shot on the Champs Elysees after the lap of honor. We started as just me and Kristin, then me, Kristin, and my mom, then me, Kristin, and her parents—until the group just grew and grew! I don't think anyone was missed, which is amazing seeing as how much of a zoo it was with all the photographers fighting to get a shot.

▲ My return to the U.S. came over 1 week later, and the city of Austin held a massive parade across town. I was startled by the huge turnout, not believing anyone back home was that interested in what I'd achieved. But I also realized my life was changing faster than I knew.

▶ I presented the former governor of Texas, George W. Bush, with one of my yellow jerseys at the state capitol.

▶▶ A suitably decorated postal truck led the parade.

▲ People of all ages showed their support as we drove down Congress Avenue. This was such a special feeling.

◄◄ One of the first things I did was to get one of my yellow jerseys framed to hang in my house. I chose the jersey I'd worn to Sestriére, my favorite memory of that first Tour win.

◄ By October, a young man named Luke David Armstrong had come into my life. It was the perfect ending to a perfect year.

LINDA ARMSTRONG KELLY
MOTHER

When Lance was born, I was 17 and fully expected a little girl. Instead, I got a rambunctious little boy with sparkling blue eyes and a serious need for speed. Though we didn't have much I saved up enough to buy a plastic three-wheeler with butterfly handlebars for Lance's second birthday. I watched him make the miraculous discovery that pushing his little feet on the pedals could move that big front wheel and that meant *go power!* He wanted to ride that thing from morning to night.

When my son was little, I worried about all the things I wasn't able to give him. Now I know what mattered most in the long run was what I was able to show him. Certain realities in our life couldn't be changed. We could sit around and cry about it, or we could find our way around the roadblocks. Our answer to every setback, sorrow, and upheaval has always been to push back, try harder, and be smarter. We weren't afraid of failing. Losing is worthwhile if you learn something from it. But quitting—that's the defeat of hope.

Now, when I watch Lance pounding up the Alps or grinding through a time trial, his eyes bloodshot and burning with resolution, I think back on the treadmill quality of our life during his early years, and I see the birth of his ability to endure—to thrive, in fact—when the terrain is at its most rugged. When things are tough, you develop this dog-with-a-bone determination to push on forward

◄ Lance and Linda Armstrong Kelly celebrate his 1993 World Championship win in Oslo, Norway.

toward something better and squeeze out every ounce of *fun* you can latch onto along the way.

The years flew, and so did my son. He had three gears: sleep, eat, and full speed ahead. Weekends were busy with bike races and swim meets. During the week, we had our routine. After a good hot breakfast, I left for work and Lance hopped on his bike and rode to school. He'd always call me when he got home, fix himself a snack, and then go for a long bike ride. After dinner, we'd go running or driving around, measuring a new bicycle course. By nine or ten, we were zonked out sleeping.

When Lance told me about IronKids, a junior triathlon that involved swimming about a thousand laps, bicycling about a thousand miles, then running farther than most people walk in a year—well, it didn't sound fun. It sounded grueling. But how can you not encourage your kids when they come to you with that look in their eyes? We brainstormed about what was needed and who could provide it. I helped him set up a rolodex of possible sponsors, and when they generously came through, I sewed their logo patches on the back of Lance's shirt and made sure he wrote them a nice thank you note. I got him a desk calendar and helped him organize his schedule. And I cheered him on. That I could do. And I'm still doing it.

After hundreds of events, including five Tour de France victories, I traveled to Europe in the summer of 2004, no less nervous and no less thrilled than I was when Lance won his first races as a teenager. My husband, Ed, and I flew into Paris and

took the train to Besançon for the second-to-last stage—a time trial that would be the defining moment. The morning newspaper featured a large photo of a jubilant Lance, along with a headline proclaiming him as the "new cannibal" who was chewing through his competitors. Ed squeezed my hand as Lance prepared to rocket down the starting ramp. My heart fluttered when I saw his face on the giant screen. He didn't look as drawn and road-weary as many of the riders did at the end of this grueling three weeks. He looked fiercely focused, but his eyes had that mischievous sparkle I love. He seemed calm, determined, and—on a fundamental level— happy. The signal was given, and Lance launched forward, bursting out with that good old *go power.*

I still love to watch him fly; agog at that energy level, loving every muscle and bone in his body. Since I was 17, I've been staring at him with that same sense of wonder. Not because he's an icon, but because he's my kid. Every mother in the world knows exactly what I'm talking about.

My son flew across the finish line in Besançon, beating the best time, winning the stage, and securing his sixth Tour de France victory. He swept me into a big, sweaty hug, but we didn't say anything. What on earth was there to say? This was his man-on-the-moon moment. He was standing on ground no other man had. In addition to the rush of love and outpouring of pride I felt as his mother, I was inspired as a human being. I felt privileged to bear witness as this amazing young man pushed back the boundaries of what is possible.

CHAPTER EIGHT

2000: A STRONG DEFENSE

★ When I came back to defend my Tour title 1 year later, I was no longer the outside challenger. I'd been in Puy de Fou. This alone had the potential to make the job of winning a second Tour even more difficult. Jan Ullrich was back as well, a factor that led some media types to declare that I would never win a Tour again. But what no one knew was the depth of my training program the previous winter and the meticulous reconnaissance we'd made of the 2000 Tour route—better, more thorough than in 1999. Even so, I was concerned about having Ullrich against me in this Tour. He was probably the only cyclist as fast as me in a time trial, and I knew his climbing had been great in the 1996, 1997, and 1998 Tours. All of which made his challenge even more exciting—I couldn't wait!

I lost the opening time trial stage to David Millar, by just 2 seconds, but I beat Ullrich by a bigger margin than that. The battle was on! Privately, I didn't rate Ullrich's chances in the mountains, and I was proved right on the very first climbing stage to Hautecam when he disappeared from the fight early on and left me to deal with Marco Pantani and Jose-Maria Jiminez. I was in Yellow again just 10 days into the race with a substantial lead over Ullrich, whose Telekom Team had already lost about 40 seconds to us in the team time trial on stage four. The Alps came next, preceded by the agonizing climb to Mont Ventoux where I rode away with Pantani and then basically gifted him the stage win. In hindsight, I regretted it enormously, but at the time I wanted to help Pantani a little since he'd had a few rotten years, both personally and professionally, and he was no threat to me overall.

I had trouble with each of the three Alpine stages. I think the verbal clash with Pantani on Mont Ventoux had affected my concentration, especially on the one to Morzine. I'd been preoccupied with chasing Pantani, who'd attacked early on in the stage, to the point I'd not taken my food bag at the day's feed station. I wasn't hungry at all and felt as strong as ever, but halfway up the final climb, the Col de la Joux-Plane, I hit the wall so badly I thought that I might have to walk to the top. I recovered a little as the climb progressed, and, luckily, Ullrich didn't really have the strength to do any real damage. It was a day I'll always remember because it could have cost me the Tour.

I made amends for my stupidity by beating Ullrich 3 days later in the closing time trial that went almost right by his home. It was only 25 seconds, but with so many Germans cheering him on, my gain was worth far more than just seconds on a timekeeper's watch. The 2000 Tour was effectively over with that ride to Mulhouse. Once again I was looking forward to Paris where I'd reunite with my family and friends and be able to thank my teammates for being so damn great! But my season had to last another month or so. The Olympics were in Sydney, and I was being pitched against Ullrich again in the individual time trial. As it turned out, neither of us was the winner this time. My U.S. Postal teammate Viatcheslav Ekimov beat both of us!

◀ TV commercials were now a part of my life in 2000, but they still placed a distant second to the importance of training and racing. This is the Nike commercial in which I'm racing a massive truck down a mountain. It's being shot in Almeria, Spain, where all those Clint Eastwood spaghetti westerns were made.

◀◀ These commercial shoots are good fun. Sometimes you even get to edit and approve some of the footage!

◀ But they are also hard work, with a team of up to 40 people working around you and expecting 100% effort.

◀◀ By 3:00 PM the filming is done and we take a quick look at the production before heading back to Nice on the private plane.

◀ My manager, Bill Stapleton (middle), always travels with me on these trips. It gives us a chance to talk business. On this one, Scott McEachern (left) came along for the ride. Scott's a great friend, as well as my representative at Nike. He follows the Tour each year with Bill.

◀ Who says you can't work hard and have fun at the same time?

▶ The Dauphiné-Libéré was that year's chosen pre-Tour stage-race, where my teammate Tyler Hamilton was in superb form. Here I am pacing him on the Col d'Izoard with 1 day to go.

A few days earlier, we'd both escaped over the Provençal hills to take a one-two into Digne-les-Bains. Next to winning a race yourself, there is no greater satisfaction than seeing a teammate—and friend—win a big race. Things looked good for my first Tour defense.

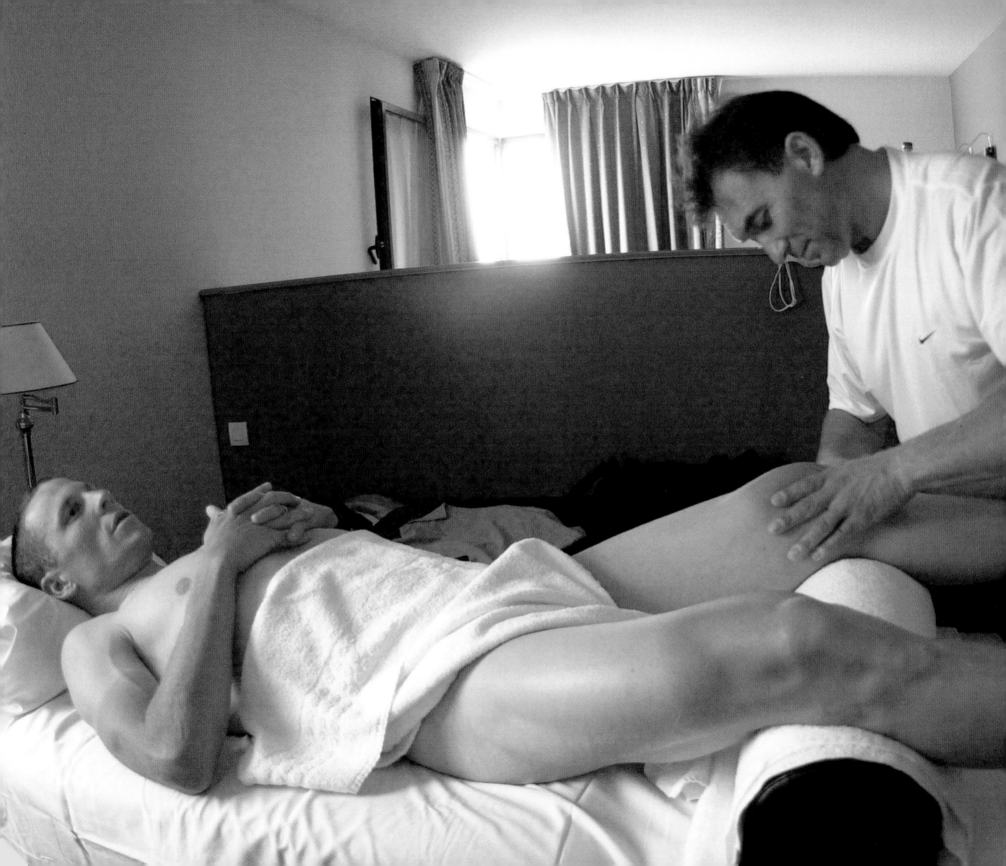

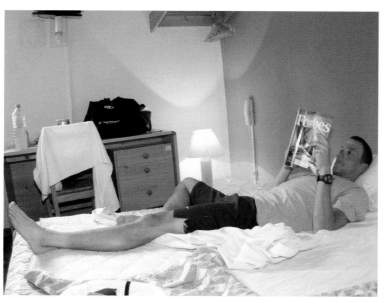

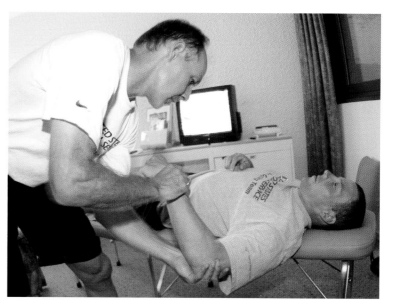

▲ Bedtime reading...Lap-top computers are banned on our team during the Tour, so I always try to get friends to buy me English-language magazines to read...stops me from going insane! As a Tour winner, I'm one of the few cyclists in the peloton who gets to have my own room in the Tour.

◄ Between racing, sleeping, and eating, a typical Tour day includes massage. It is a time for physical relaxation as well as the chance to pass a few quiet moments with your soigneur. Freddy Viane was with me at Motorola, and I asked him to come back to this team for the 2000 season. He is a great masseur and someone who I can totally relax with after a stage.

► Jeff Spencer, my chiropractor, travels each and every day with the team. He is there primarily for me, but he also helps other team members who may need some gentle manipulation after a long, hot day in the saddle.

▲ The opening 11-kilometer stage of the 2000 Tour was made for me, but I came in second to Britain's David Millar. Any disappointment I felt was washed away the next day, and I was the first to congratulate Millar, who has the potential for even greater things one day.

▲ Next target was the team time trial to St. Nazaire but we came second! I really wanted to win this stage, as I'd come so close in Motorola's days. But team policy dictated that we hold back after strong winds blew the squad to bits on the St. Nazaire bridge. ONCE were the winners, not for the first time in Tour history.

▲ It is the eve of the Pyrenees, and the press are starting to ask why I am not yet in Yellow after 10 days of racing. Is there a problem, they ask?

◄ Each morning we held a team meeting in the little team truck before the stage begins. It is Johan who lays down the law, explaining in incredible detail what to expect, how the racing will probably go, where the wind will be coming from, where to place ourselves in the peloton. There's always tension at these meetings—effectively, we are about to go to war on our rivals. This can be seen on our faces, George Hincapie and myself, as Johan does his stuff.

◄◄ **PREVIOUS SPREAD**
We were right back to where we wanted to be now, leading and
controlling the Tour on the approach to the Alps. Mont Ventoux is
on this day's horizon as we ride past lavender fields in Provençe.

▲ Marco Pantani wins the Mont Ventoux stage with me right there
with him. In hindsight, I was very naïve to not react to Pantani's last
acceleration as we came around the final turn.

▲ The two of us were at it again 3 days later on the final climb
to Courchevel. This time I didn't have the strength to go with Pantani
when he made his move 6 kilometers from the line. He attacked so fast
that it would have been suicidal to try and keep pace. Even so, Pantani's
style of racing had unsettled me, and it affected my morale and
concentration for the coming stage in the Alps.

▲ On stage sixteen, I had the team chasing Pantani for ages after he
attacked on the Col des Saisies. But by the time we got to the final
climb, the Col de Joux-Plane, Pantani had abandoned and I was starting
to regret the efforts I'd made earlier. Jan Ullrich sensed I was in trouble
and was starting to make life difficult. Richard Virenque, too, sensed
I was not at my best.

  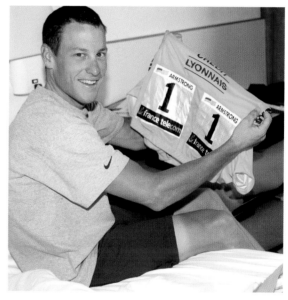

▲ It was a nightmare situation for me. I'd hit the wall less than halfway up the Joux-Plane, drained of any energy and strength after my obsessive reaction to Pantani's attack. It looks like a horrible image—the Yellow Jersey suffering so much—but, in fact, I remember very little about it at the time. Only later did I realize how close I'd come to blowing the whole race on that one climb. As it was, I kept my deficit to Ullrich within 2 minutes on the stage. The Tour was still well within reach.

▲ This was a ritual I enjoyed more than usual on the morning after my collapse on the Joux-Plane. Sticking my race numbers on a freshly laundered Yellow Jersey brought home to me the responsibility I was carrying—and to not waste such a valuable commodity in the future. I was now just 5 days from Paris, and 3 days short of another rendezvous with Ullrich—the final time trial that began in Germany and ended in France.

◄◄◄ Troyes was the scene for an unusual ceremony on the last day of the race. I was measured for my own weight in champagne before the special train took the riders into the French capital.

◄ We rode into Paris on the famed Orient Express, one of the original ones complete with wooden carriages and crystal-glass lighting. Johan and I had our own compartment where we could relax and enjoy a glass of champagne on the way in—just one glass.

◄◄◄ I had a double escort on the Champs Elysees. First, Dirk DeMol, the assistant director of the U.S. Postal Team, and Johan Bruyneel helped smooth my passage to a second Tour with a regular supply of tactical advice and encouragement—the likes of which I would never have received from anyone else.

◄ Frankie Andreu ended his career on the Champs Elysees. He is an old friend from the early Motorola days, and his retirement was unexpected and a little sad for me. But, typically, Frankie was the first to reach for the tray of champagne awaiting us after the lap of honor.

◄ All thoughts of Marco Pantani, the Alps, and the Col de Joux-Plane went out the window as I began the 58-kilometer time trial from Fribourg. This was Jan Ullrich's home territory. We passed so close to his home, and I wanted to really set the record straight about which of us was the fastest. Ullrich had missed the 1999 Tour due to an injury, and I'd heard that there were a lot of people saying my time trials were weak! Consequently, I put 25 seconds into Ullrich by the finish, which silenced just about everyone. I remember this time trial for my total concentration and for the hundreds of thousands of Germans who lined the road to Mulhouse, applauding me as strongly as Ullrich. They really were a sporting crowd, especially since I'd probably just humiliated their hero.

▲ Luke was the first to greet me on the podium after the race.
Someone had decked him out in a miniature yellow jersey!
My expression says everything about how I felt—
exuberant would be an understatement.

◄ Then it was the turn of team owner Thom Weisel to ride along with me for a few minutes.
Thom had been the man who persuaded the USPS to sponsor me in 1998, and my second
Tour victory helped repay him even more for his belief. I was extremely happy for him.
Everyone on the team deserved this victory.

▲ My bronze-medal ride in the Olympics Time Trial was perhaps a good performance, considering my training accident in Nice, but I was disappointed all the same. The road race had been a complete fiasco with our radio sets not working properly. None of us even knew that Ullrich had gone up the road with two Telekom teammates! The time trial was a chance to restore American pride, but I just didn't have it on that day and had to take a backseat to Ullrich and the gold medallist, Viatcheslav Ekimov, who at least came from the same trade team as me.

▲ It was tough being on the bottom step of the Olympic podium, but I was genuinely pleased for Eki, as he had worked so hard for me and the team all year long. I think Ullrich was at least as disappointed as me, if not more—for had he gone one better than his silver medal, it would have been an unforgettable "double" for the new Olympic Road Champion.

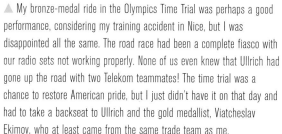

◀ I might look good and aggressive in this shot during the summer classic—the Championship of Zurich—but, in fact, I was recovering from a serious training crash and was not sure if I could do a good ride at the Olympic Games. The Zurich race is tough, held on a hilly, twisting circuit and always under extremely hot conditions. I felt good enough by the end to say yes to the Olympic selectors. I would go to Sydney.

CHRIS CARMICHAEL
LONG TIME PERSONAL COACH

In 1990, people told me about this kid, a first-year amateur who possessed the raw talent that could make him a champion. I was encouraged even though I had neither seen nor spoken to him yet. Lance Armstrong was headstrong and confident for his age, traits some people found challenging but just what I was looking for.

We met for the first time during a layover in Chicago's O'Hare International Airport. I was on my way home from Europe with the A Team of the U.S. National Cycling Team, and Lance was on his way to Sweden with the National B Team.

"Why didn't I get selected to the A Team trip?" he snapped.

"I didn't select the team," I told him. "I was hired after the selections were made. But now that I'm here, if you want to be on the A Team, you have to prove yourself to me."

"There's no doubt that in a really short period of time, you'll see I deserve to be on the A Team."

"Fine, prove it to me."

"OK. Done."

That was it. We went our separate ways, and I didn't give the conversation much thought. I didn't see Lance as difficult, arrogant, or brash. He was just a kid racing with older guys and looking to get ahead. During that trip to Sweden, Lance finished seventh in a Pro-Am stage-race against some pretty heavy hitters. I asked him for proof and he delivered.

◀ Chris Carmichael enjoying a rare bike ride with Lance Armstrong at the Ride of the Roses weekend, 2003

During the 1991 Tour DuPont, I introduced Lance to Jim Ochowicz, the director of the Motorola Cycling Team. Jim was interested in Lance and we worked out a deal. Lance would ride for Motorola but remain an amateur until after the Barcelona Olympics. When Lance headed off to meet his new Motorola Team, I told Lance I had enjoyed working with him and wished him luck, and he replied, "This doesn't change anything. You're still my coach." I nodded my head, figuring there might be some kind of transition period before he settled in with the pro team. Within weeks, I started getting phone calls late at night from Lance, who was already contemplating quitting. After finishing last in the Clasica San Sebastian, we were on the phone for 2-plus hours. The next week there was another long, late-night phone call, but this time it was after he finished second at the Championship of Zurich.

Being close to Lance Armstrong through cancer, from the beginning all the way through the darkest days when each conversation with him could have been my last, we forged a bond that goes way beyond a typical coach-athlete relationship. It was the strength of that bond that allowed me to convince him he needed to get back to training.

Lance's first comeback to the professional peloton was extremely challenging for me and forever changed my coaching methods. While Lance was physically prepared, there were emotional issues we hadn't dealt with, and they surfaced upon his return to Europe. Within 2 months, he was ripping his race numbers off during a rainy stage of Paris–Nice. He was finished, going home, never riding again, playing golf, didn't need this crap.

Despite all the images that have been captured of Lance, there is no photographic record of the moment he put it all together in his head. Somewhere on the slopes of Beech Mountain, climbing alone in the mist and pouring rain, he realized he had a second chance, a gift, and the best way to honor that second chance was to work his ass off and become the world's best cyclist. It would be his way to show to the world that cancer could be beaten and to provide hope to cancer patients in their darkest days. I was driving a car next to him, slamming my hand on the door and yelling, "Allez, allez, Lance. Go!" I wish you could have seen it, and yet, I'm glad you didn't. I'm glad there's no photograph from that moment and that I had the honor of being the only witness.

Going into the 2004 Tour de France, I knew Lance was in great shape, but I also knew it would take more than great fitness to secure a record-setting sixth Tour de France victory. Four champions before him had arrived at the Tour with the great conditioning and the same opportunity, yet none of them wore yellow in Paris for a sixth time. The morning of the prologue, I saw in Lance the crucial element that would tip the balance in his favor. He possessed the volatile mixture of excitement, eager anticipation, and the spark of determination. When the mixture's right, you get an explosive performance like the one we all had the honor of witnessing for those three weeks in July.

CHAPTER NINE

2001: YEAR OF CONSOLIDATION

★ By the end of the 2000 season, my team and I felt that we had perfected my buildup for a Tour defense that needed little change. But change we did in 2001, substituting the Dauphiné-Libéré stage-race in June with the equally testing Tour of Switzerland that ended just a few weeks before the Tour began. The reason was made clear early on in the season—there was an uphill time trial in the Swiss race that would give me the ideal preparation for a similarly difficult stage in the Tour. Normally, the Dauphiné follows a similar route as the Tour's Alpine stages, but not this year. So this was another reason to miss the French race after a few years.

The plan went well, with me winning the opening prologue in style, leading the race for 2 days, and then kicking back until the time trial up to Crans-Montana. I won that, too, taking back the Yellow Jersey for good with just a few stages in the mountains left to race. Without Jan Ullrich to compete against, my opposition came down to Waldimir Belli and Gilberto Simoni—two Italians still riding strongly just a week or so after the end of the Giro d'Italia. Ullrich had also ridden the Giro that May, and I'd heard impressive reports about his gradual return to form in the last week. Until then, he'd been very low key.

He was still my most feared opponent as the Tour began, with an 8.2-kilometer prologue, but my third place there already put me ahead of him in the psychological stakes. The team time trial put me farther in front with the first mountain stage just 4 days away. But then the Telekom and U.S. Postal Teams got into a war of words when they let an escape group gain 36 minutes on a soaking wet stage toward the Alps. Still angry with Telekom for not helping us chase on that eighth stage, we played a particularly bad joke on them, with me feigning a bad day in the saddle as the tough climbs began on stage ten. They really thought I was in trouble and sent all their workers to the front at one point, wasting needless energy and giving me an armchair ride to the foot of the last climb, the Alpe d'Huez. It was here that the sting was played out when I suddenly swept past a hopeful Ullrich on the wheel of Jose Luis Rubiera, who was perhaps our most intelligent teammate, and then jumped away in an attack that would gain me almost 2 full minutes on Ullrich!

There were now two Tours being fought—me against Ullrich and the two of us against André Kivilev and Francois Simon, who were the two greatest beneficiaries of that crazy escape on stage eight. I got another minute on my rival in the Chamrousse time trial the following day, but the Pyrenees was the sweeter prize, for both of us had to race flat out to take the time out of Kivilev and Simon—and it was hurting Ullrich more than it was hurting me. Stage twelve gained me 23 seconds, while stage thirteen was worth another minute. Suddenly I was back in the Yellow Jersey after racing for 2 weeks in my blue team colors—it felt great! I think both Ullrich and I had really enjoyed this Tour. It had brought out the very best in both of us and he offered a sporting handshake as we crossed the line together at Luz-Ardiden.

◀ The team's training camp in Phoenix, Arizona, was a good time for me to meet the media again. Contact with the media is a very important part of my work, and it is a lot easier in the quieter atmosphere of the camp than at some race where there are too many other competing considerations.

▲ The penultimate stage was a really tough one, ending on a mountain about 4,000 feet above sea level. But I prefer this race when there is also a time trial to contend. Hill training can come later.

▲ Earlier in March, I'd lined up for the Tour of Murcia alongside my two greatest rivals of recent years—Jan Ullrich and Marco Pantani. The organizers were delighted all three of us were at the start, but I think we would much rather have got on with the racing and not been made to pose next to each other so uncomfortably—the Tour was still 4 months away!

◄ The Catalonia region of Spain has some great hills on which to train and race. That's why I chose to move to Girona. It is also the battleground for the Semana Catalana, and I'm seen here on stage one to Las Rosas, testing my legs against the rest of the boys to see how I feel. I feel good!

▲ I was never really troubled in the Tour of Switzerland and used it as a high-level training ride for the Tour. But I still prefer the tougher Dauphiné, as the organizers nearly always make a point of taking the race over many of the same roads that the Tour will use in July.

▲ Yes, the podium girls are almost as pretty as the Swiss scenery but maybe I am smiling at the thought of race-organizer Tony Rominger having to fly the team and me across the Alps to St Moritz and our final pre-Tour training camp. A good friend, Rominger promised me that if I won the Swiss race, he would personally pay for the helicopter ride from Lausanne. He delivered as any honest Swiss man would, and it saved us a drive of over 6 hours after the finish.

◀ The Tour of Switzerland is one of the toughest and most prestigious stage-races in the world, and the cobbled ascent of the St. Gotthard Pass is one of the sport's toughest climbs.

◄ The obligatory pre-Tour press conference in Dunkirk gave me an early chance to put matters right for the team.
We were still under official investigation for an alleged use of prohibited drugs in the 2000 Tour, and I went to great lengths—
to a partially deaf audience of unbelieving journalists—to make it clear there was no case to answer. I also wanted to make it clear
the U.S. Postal Team came to win another Tour, and that Jan Ullrich was, once again, my most feared rival.

▲ Sometimes it is risky to stop for a pee when the racing is on.
This is where my more loyal teammates come into play—though not literally!

►This is what a Tour peloton can look like when the big teams make a move. We are on stage four, heading south out of Belgium to Verdun,
with 24 hours to the team time trial. This is always a nervous stage, and we are at the front putting psychological pressure on the ONCE
and Festina Teams by riding hard into a crosswind. In the end, the racing quiets down, and Laurent Jalabert has a great stage-win.

▲ The scene as Heras and Vandervelde picked themselves up. It was too early in the Tour to leave such important men behind. We had no choice but to wait. Luckily, they weren't too badly hurt.

▲ Stage eight was a wet one, a very wet one. I spent a lot of it trying to get my radio to work, which might have partially accounted for a break getting away with a massive lead of 35 minutes. That might be why I don't look too pleased.

◀ Another team time trial, another big disappointment. The rain-soaked stage to Bar le Duc went to Credit-Agricole after we've had a heart-stopping fall involving Christian Vandervelde and Roberto Heras. But for that fall and the lost time while we all waited for them, I think we would have won the stage for the first time in our lives.

▲ We had Telekom fooled on stage ten, and they worked like Trojans on the Col de la Madeleine. But I had the last laugh, attacking Ullrich at the foot of Alpe d'Huez and building a big lead by the finish. This is me in full flight 2 kilometers from the end.

▶ I am ecstatic. I have just nearly made the fastest ascent of Alpe d'Huez and won the stage. Just look at those biceps! I've also taken big chunks out of the overall lead of Simon, who deposed O'Grady as race leader on this stage.

▶▶ Another clinically perfect ride the next day has taken even more time out of Simon, who has just 5 minutes of his overall lead to play with. More importantly, I have clocked the fastest time at the Chamrousse ski station and beaten Ullrich by exactly 1 minute.

▲◀ In the last few kilometers, stage twelve saw Jan and me dueling. This was becoming a great Tour, as we both had to really go for it to overtake Simon (and Kivilev, who was the real danger man, I thought).

▲ Jan crashed the next day on the descent of the Col du Peyresourde, but I have waited for him. It seems like the right thing to do at the time. We are back together as the final climb to Pla d'Adet begins, but soon I will attack. I have to attack.

◀ At last, I'm in the Yellow Jersey for the first time in this Tour and can afford to smile easier.

◄ It would have been easy to relax a little before Paris, but there was still the time trial to Saint-Amand-Montrond that, as race leader, I was obliged to try and win. It's a question of pride, really. It was a perfect course for me, with a mixture of undulating straight roads and sharp, twisty corners. As such, I put another 1'40" into Ullrich to bring my overall lead up to a very safe 6'44".

▲ But the heat had taken its toll on me, and I felt just a little faint on the podium. Bernard Hinault shows concern.

▲ And a greeting to my friend, Pierre Guiberol, a member of the Garde Republicaine, which escorts the Tour around France. Pierre, an English-speaking official, got to know me way back in the early days of Motorola. He is a friend well worth having.

▶ The four jersey winners pose in Paris. Laurent Jalabert (far left), Erik Zabel (middle), Oscar Sevilla (far right), and I are the men who matter!

▶▶ As always, there are LAF fans all around the Champs Elysees circuit.

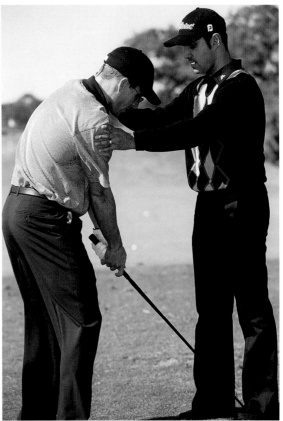

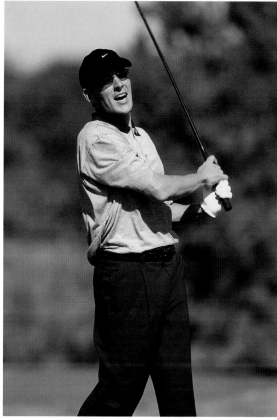

◄◄◄◄ Back in the U.S., after my season is truly over, I host the Lance Armstrong Golf Invitational in Austin, Texas. It's a fun weekend that raises big money for the foundation and gives a chance for friends and sponsors to play a round of golf with me, for what that's worth! Here, I am presenting an award to Dick Moran of Trek Bicycles, with the help of Butch Harmon, renowned coach of Tiger Woods.

◄◄◄ Butch has a son, Claude, who is a pro golfer. As you can see, I'm in need of his expert instruction. I have since retired from golf!

◄◄ It seems golf is all about having fun.

◄ The infamous Armstrong drive and follow through.

JEFF GARVEY
FOUNDING CHAIRMAN OF THE LANCE ARMSTRONG FOUNDATION

I first met Lance just as he was coming out of chemotherapy in the winter of 1997. He was completely bald at the time but, having lost both of my parents to cancer, his appearance didn't shock me like it may have others. On meeting him, I was shocked to discover how much he knew about me, or more to the point, my company, Austin Ventures. I was a successful venture capitalist, and my company had helped launch many sound businesses. It seemed Lance had already had a dream to build the Lance Armstrong Foundation (LAF), almost before he'd even ended having treatment for the awful disease. We formally met over lunch at my Austin home, and I was immediately taken by Lance's attitude to our meeting. He was prepared, knew the lay of the land, and wanted to be competitive in our conversation. Essentially, the very same characteristics so evident in how he races the Tour every July!

In fact the idea of creating the LAF had come in a previous meeting between Lance, Bart Knaggs, Bill Stapleton, and John Korioth over beers and a Mexican dinner a few months earlier. Their ideas came close to my vision of what the LAF could achieve if handled properly. In my 30 years of business success, nothing has provided me with true and lasting fulfilment like the LAF, and we are now the most successful grant-making, nonprofit organization focused exclusively on the needs of cancer survivors.

It wasn't until October of 1998 that I actually

◀ Jeff Garvey with Lance in Austin, Texas, 2001.
A successful businessman, Garvey helped Lance
to create the LAF during his recovery from cancer in 1997.

saw Lance race. My wife and I went to the World Championships in Valkenburg, Holland, and saw Lance and his rivals race for over 6 hours under torrential rain, wind, and cold. I was impressed! I remember putting my head down in a silent prayer that Lance might just win as they climbed the last hill—he didn't, but was stellar in defeat. Since then I have been to every one of his five victorious Tours de France, where my role is as a supportive friend and unofficial time-keeper. In 1999, I followed the first time trial of the race in Johan Bruyneel's car, calculating the time splits as Lance's actual times were shouted across at me from Johan's radio/TV. I'd then pass the figures back to Johan who'd relay them on to Lance. I became something of a good-luck charm, because Lance insisted that I follow him in as many time trials as possible. My record is good: four stage-wins out of five attempts!

The worst experience for me was the Pornic–Nantes time trial in the 2003 Tour. It was torturous, with terrible weather all day long before Lance went off at 4:06 PM. We'd all been hanging around in the pouring rain, too nervous to hold proper conversations, too wet and cold to think of anything else but Lance's chances against Ullrich. The first 15 minutes of that car ride that day were as intense, scary, and dangerous as all of my previous driving experiences put together. I can honestly say I never took my right hand off the passenger door handle until we got word on TV that Ullrich had crashed.

Thankfully, Lance began to cruise toward the finish once he, too, had heard the news and the tension in the car returned almost to normal for such a day. The road widened with about 4 kilometers to go, and we were able to draw even with him on the right-hand side. Lance looked over at us and did his famous "finger flick," with his right hand never leaving the drop! This has become something of a tradition between him and Johan, but it was my first sighting and it now signified a fifth Tour victory—as long as he could stay upright. I was one of the happiest men alive that afternoon as Lance pulled on his Yellow Jersey. He had been the ONLY man in the peloton who had ridden the course that morning for reconnaissance. It is that focus and willingness to go beyond the "call of duty" that makes Lance such an incredible champion.

I think the 2004 Tour victory was his easiest and most controlled of the six, which speaks loudly for the quality of his team and the genius of Johan. I was in the car at Besançon for the final time trial. The suspense level was very high because anything could happen. To say that Lance rode aggressively would be an understatement!

The celebration parade in Austin was spectacular—different than in 1999, the last time we had one for Lance. He actually rode a mountain bike from the Auditorium Shores to the Capital alongside the mayor of Austin and a few other notable politicians. There is no doubt that the people of Austin, Texas, love this guy and for good reason.

CHAPTER TEN

2002: MY BEST TOUR YET

★ When I look back on my career one day in the future, there will be many questions to answer. Which was my greatest win? Who was my greatest opponent? What was my greatest team? What was my favorite race? But I don't need to wait until I retire to tell you that 2002 was my best Tour ever, that it was my most satisfying, and that it was my easiest to win. Okay, so there was no Jan Ullrich, no climber like Marco Pantani to bother me, and the course was as perfect as one could be for me. But the fact is I was better trained than I'd been since winning that first Tour in 1999.

I'd come to Europe a little later than normal, by just a few weeks, in late February. But I'd trained better in the winter than for many a year and felt so good I turned down the chance of racing in the Vuelta a Murcia and went training even more. I then pulled off the very satisfying deed of riding the 300-kilometer Milan–San Remo as my first race and was so strong near the end that I made it over the Poggio in the front group and ended in the same time as winner Mario Cipollini. So things looked good as early as the middle of March, and April would see me riding the cobbled classics of Belgium for the first time since 1995. I was there to try and motivate George Hincapie and to see if my presence might push him that bit farther and win himself a classic like the Tour of Flanders. In the end George did not win Flanders, Ghent–Wevelgem, or Paris–Roubaix—but I'd had a couple of great outings to savor—even if I scared myself (and Johan!) close to death on some of those cobbled tracks!

Liège–Bastogne–Liège was also on my program for the first time since 1996, as well as a regular favorite, the Amstel Gold Race. I hope one day to finally win this great race, but fourth was all I could get in 2002. To be honest, I need a harder course than even this hilly classic provided me. Races continued to come—the G.P. Midi Libre was new to me but that didn't stop me from winning it without too much trouble, while the Dauphiné-Libéré was a great deal harder, but ended in the same satisfying result. I knew I was more ready for the Tour than I'd been in years and would be able to win it comfortably if nothing went wrong.

And nothing did. A prologue win in Luxembourg set me on the right path, and yet another second place in the team time trial proved the postal boys were as strong as ever. By stage eleven, I was in Yellow after winning at La Mongie and won again the very next day at Plateau de Beille, putting more and more time into my closest adversary, Joseba Beloki. The Mont Ventoux stage went to Richard Virenque, but I gained even more time on Beloki after his failed attack with 7 kilometers to go. At that point, the Tour was virtually over, with six stages to go. The remaining Alpine stages came and went without any drama, yet more time was taken from Beloki, and I ended the Tour in Paris a massive 7'17" ahead of him—just 20 seconds short of my biggest-ever winning advantage in the 1999 Tour.

◁ I was in this long race to try and help George Hincapie get a decent chance in the finale, but also to get some race mileage into my legs. Here, George and I are descending the Passo del Turchino, heading for the Riviera coastline.

▲ Next stop on the get-in-shape trail was the Criterium Internationale in northern France. I took a virtual Tour team with me to this race. Here we are saluting the crowds before the start of the opening stage

◀ Everything depended on the closing time trial, as always, and I gave it my very best shot. A Basque, Alberto Martinez, beat me by just 1/100th of a second! I was bummed, but also realized I had good form for this time of the year.

▲ The opening kilometers gave me a chance to catch up with an old friend, Axel Merckx. When I was living in Nice, we'd often socialize together. It was nice to catch up.

▲ I opted to race in many of the Belgian classics in 2002, again, to help George Hincapie a little bit. But Liège-Bastogne-Liège was for myself, which is why I was angry to miss the break, and then have half the Telekom Team sitting on me whenever I chased. Payback time for the Tours of recent years, I suppose!

▲ I then rode the Midi Libre for the first time that spring and came out of it in good shape, despite the torrential rain on some of the days. It's not always a glamorous life!

▲ Here I am, in yellow, sprinting for the line on the last stage, with Christophe Moreau and Igor DeGaldeano in contention.

◄ One week later was the Amstel Gold Race in Holland. I love racing this hilly classic, but each year the odds seem stacked against me. In 2002, it was no different. But I was satisfied with my form and not too disappointed to finish fourth behind winner Michele Bartoli.

▲ This had been a busy season so far—but I was in great shape for the Dauphiné-Libéré, which I wanted to win for the first time in my career. Here, I'm leading Kivilev, Zubeldia, amd Moreau up the grueling Mont Ventoux on stage two.

▶ Stage six was the tough one—a six-mountain epic that ended in Morzine after the Col de la Joux-Plane. I'm attacking all the time now, trying to build a decent lead, trying to test myself to the maximum—but it took me forever to shake off Andrei Kivilev, a respected rival on the Cofidis Team. When Kivilev was killed one year later in Paris–Nice, I was devastated, as I considered him a very talented man and a friend. I'd hoped that he would one day become a teammate on the U.S. Postal Team.

▲ Victory on stage six of the Dauphiné was a good indication of my form with 3 weeks still to go. I felt stronger than I've ever been.

◀ *Le Train Bleu*—I was absolutely delighted at how my team performed in the Dauphiné. But tough decisions now had to be made to select the Tour riders. I confer with Johan on everything, but the final choice is never easy as, effectively, we could field two decent teams in the Tour.

The Dauphiné-Libéré is not just a great race. It is also a very beautiful one. Each year the organizers use roads relatively unknown in the Alps with scenery to match.

▶ In Luxembourg, I won my first Tour prologue since 1999 at the Puy de Fou. It was a good sign!

▲ Charly Gaul, Luxembourg's greatest cyclist, greeted me on the podium, and I presented him with the polka-dot jersey, which I had also won that day. Gaul is one of the last surviving greats of our sport. You can see him in many of those old black-and-white shots that fill history books.

▶ After a spring of helping George Hincapie, it was now his turn to protect me from the winds on stage one. We kept the jersey that day but, in the best traditions of the Tour, managed to lose it on stage two into Sarrebroucken. Our minds were on winning more than the team time trial in two days' time.

► Another team time trial, another second place! This time it was ONCE who got the better of us by just 16 seconds. But we finished as a complete team, whereas ONCE lost two riders in their desperate attempt to win, which is an important observation when you consider there was still over 2 weeks to go. They'd now have to control the race all the way to the Pyrenees.

▶ Second place again—this time on stage nine to and from Lorient. Botero had beaten me for the second time this season, and I was far from pleased with my form that day.

▶▶ But I had time to encourage my friend David Millar, who was having a bad Tour so far. He then went on to win a stage 3 days later!

▶▶▶ Stage eleven saw a big fight on the last climb to La Mongie, where myself and Heras rode all over Joseba Beloki in our quest to take both the stage and the Yellow Jersey. I won the stage, but it could so easily have been Roberto who won.

▶▶▶▶ The Plateau de Beille was a sweet victory. I attacked a long way out, about 8 kilometers, and paced myself perfectly to the finish, with a time gain of over 1 minute on Beloki. Strangely, this was only my second-ever Tour road stage win while wearing the Yellow Jersey.

◀ We were completely in control as the race traversed Provençe under a scorching hot sun on stage fourteen. I'm checking distances and location on a small card everyone carries with them in the Tour. The Mont Ventoux was today's obstacle, and I wanted to make sure the day's early escape didn't get too far ahead—in it was Richard Virenque.

▲ On the Ventoux, Jose Luis Rubiera is doing great work. But Virenque takes this stage.

◄▲ But then Beloki attacks, making me mad.
I dropped him immediately and set off up the exposed
mountain thinking only of the time gain over the Basque.
At the finish, I was now 4'21" ahead of him on overall time.
He'll think twice about attacking next time.

► Another day in Yellow.
Another smile. By stage sixteen,
I felt the Tour was very much
going my way, and I could afford
to relax a little.

◄ This was one of those rare days when I had a chance to enjoy the stunning scenery. Here we are gently climbing up the Col du Lautaret on our way to the mighty Col du Galibier and an eventual finish at La Plagne. I took more time out of Beloki there but finished well over 1 minute behind the stage winner, Michael Boogerd.

◄◄ There are more and more American fans coming to the Tour each year, and some of them are quite amazing characters. This guy is running ahead of us on the Col de la Colombiére. I think people like him must train at altitude, especially for the Tour!

◄ After three relatively quiet days in the Alps, I let rip in the closing time trial to Macon, winning by 53 seconds from Raimundas Rumsas, who assured himself of third place overall that day. For 4 years now, I'd not lost the last time trial of the Tour.

 On the last stage, I had my picture taken with the last man in the 2002 Tour de France, Ikor Florez. It was his idea.

▶ Last-day antics were again stifled a little by another battle for the Green Jersey, but Johan and I still squeezed in a glass or two of champagne.

◀ The final podium of the 2002 Tour and I'm posing happily with Beloki and Rumsas. This was definitely the easiest Tour of my career. I had over 7 minutes on Beloki and another minute on Rumsas. If only it would be this easy in 2003!

▲ This post-race interview was an enjoyable one. I'd had the easiest Tour of my life and won by a huge margin—a good reason to smile!

BILL STAPLETON
LONG TIME AGENT/MANAGER

Over the past 9 years, I have spent a great deal of time with Lance. I met him as a young superstar athlete in 1995 looking for an agent and manager (but, in typical Lance style, not sure he even needed one). He gave me a shot when he had much safer, much larger (and probably much better) options and I will never forget that. Since then, we've both seen a lot. Back then, there were no big endorsement deals. There was no Nike, no Coca-Cola, no Subaru, no Bristol Myers-Squibb. There were no books, no *Sports Illustrated* awards, no White House visits. Somehow, Lance and I have stayed together as friends and business partners through enormous changes in our lives: he got sick, we both had kids, our worlds both got more and more complicated. I think that's rare but, with Lance, it makes sense. Through it all, Lance has remained unaffected by his stardom. Lance's experiences and fame have made him a better person, not some spoiled rock star that so many of us might have become. He believes in the same things today that he did before he beat cancer or rode down the Champs Elysees in yellow: Loyalty. Hard Work. Results. Straight Talk. Those words define Lance. They are what make him such a great person and a great partner.

A number of things make Lance an indisputably rare human being. First, Lance is true to himself. I have never met anyone who is more honest with himself than he is. He does not kid himself, ever. Second, he's absolutely hilarious. He possesses an

◀ Bill Stapleton with Lance in Spain, 2000

uncanny ability to speak in convincing dialects in many different languages. Go to Australia with Lance and he's suddenly straight out of the Outback, go to Paris and he's a chain-smoking Frenchman, go to Canada and he's a hoser. He simply loves to laugh, he loves to make fun of his friends (and be made fun of), and he just genuinely loves life. Third, Lance is a great business partner: He communicates when there are issues that need honest discussion, he says thanks for a job well done, and he is as fair-minded as anyone I have ever met. And, finally, Lance is the toughest son of a bitch I have ever met. He drives everyone around him like he drives himself, he expects performance and results, and he suffers no fools.

By the summer of 2003, I honestly thought I really knew and understood Lance. But, what he did that July was something so amazing that even those of us who know him well were astonished at his resolve. Let's face it: Lance was not, physically, the best rider in that Tour. He may not have been in the top four. And, emotionally, Lance was different. He was shaken, he was quiet, he was tired, he was indifferent. His face looked drained. His ubiquitous sense of humor was absent. His edge was gone. Even worse, there was an impending feeling that something bad was going to happen each day.

We had all gotten accustomed to waltzing into Paris with 5 minutes to spare. We just weren't used to Lance not making it look easy. We didn't know exactly what to say or do. So, we just supported him, encouraged him. I have seen many athletes under

pressure and I believe that there are only a handful that would not have cracked that summer. The Tour is 3 weeks long. There is so much downtime to recover and think; so much time to consider, to analyze, to question, and to doubt. Most of us would have caved in quietly: a flat tire, a cold, a stomach bug. Our fear of losing would have manifested itself in some way like that. But not so with Lance. He dug in—he remembered puking his guts out from chemo, he remembered apple fritters, he thought about all those cancer patients sitting in La-Z-Boys—and then he dug deeper. He just kept thinking that he needed one good day. And, on Luz-Ardiden, he had one good day.

In 2004, Lance raced so well in the Prologue at Liège. He didn't win, but that didn't matter—he was taking command again, and that's what counted. By stage twelve, I felt Lance was going to win. We were all scared a crazy fan might hurt him or a bad crash might take him out of contention, but it was not to be. He'd dealt with some serious family problems in 2003 but came back stronger and more focused than I'd ever seen him. He seemed to be relishing the daily grind of suffering and training again.

Lance is a man totally unafraid of failure. Yes, he always wants to win but, if he does fail (on even the grandest of stages), he is pissed off for a few days and then simply moves on to the next big adventure. Because he is not afraid to fail and because he knows there are no second chances, he is willing to invest everything to win. No excuses. That, in my opinion, is a man with life by the ball.

◀ That summer, I opted to ride the Clasica San Sebastian for the first time in quite a few years. Even though I was due to return to the States in a few weeks, I still enjoyed opening up the lungs with yet another race. This one's a hard one. A course that includes the tough climb of the Jaizkibel.

▲ One last race in 2002, the G.P. Eddy Merckx in Belgium. I chose Viatcheslav Ekimov as my partner in that event, partly because I knew he wouldn't set a ridiculously high pace for me to follow! Ekimov is also the reigning Olympic Time Trial Champion. The two of us were quite a draw for Eddy Merckx. I was more than happy to ride this event one more time.

▶ The day after the Zuri-Metzgete, I visited the World Cycling Centre in Aigle, Switzerland, and met an array of children training and studying to be top cyclists themselves. There's a superb indoor track there, as well as a gymnasium and even normal school rooms. I was impressed.

CHAPTER ELEVEN

2003: A HARD-EARNED FIVE

⭐ What a contrast in 2003! My Tour-winning advantage this time was a mere 1'01", and the man whom I'd only just managed to beat was the old warrior himself, Mr Ullrich. In 2002, I had little to worry about in the mountains. But in 2003, I had two, three, and four climbers ranged against me, including Iban Mayo, the most aggressive and determined of them all. Whereas 2002 was a Tour with little or no mishap at all, 2003 was like a battlefield each and every day—and I was the main target. In hindsight, it is hard to know whether I was very lucky to make it to Paris at all, or unlucky enough to have had so much get in my way. I certainly enjoyed the 2003 Tour far less than the previous ones, but that goes without saying, for my personal life off the bike had interrupted my concentration and moral preparation for the Tour. The result speaks for itself.

Until the start of the Tour, my season had gone almost exactly as planned with a full winter's buildup leading to my near-habitual season's start at the Vuelta a Murcia in the first week of March. I was in good shape then and had built the foundation to try and win Liège-Bastogne-Liège over 1 month later. Unfortunately, I overestimated my strength, handing control of the race to my rivals. My huge disappointment with wasting yet another opportunity in Liège was diluted somewhat by seeing my friend, rival, and ex-teammate Tyler Hamilton win his first-ever Classic.

The Tour reconnaissance went well, with successful camps in both the Alps and Pyrenees, to the point where everything seemed on target as I began the Dauphiné-Libéré the first weekend of June. If I could point to a period in the season when I felt it was suddenly going wrong, it was in this highly competitive French race that I was trying to win for the second consecutive time.

Whether it was the stage five crash, where I fell on a mountain descent at over 70 kilometers per hour, or the battering I was getting from an excessively ambitious Iban Mayo, I may never know. But it led to a bad final month's preparation, compared with other years. July 2003 was to become the most challenging period of my sporting life. I've no doubt that if 2003 had been only my second Tour defense, I might have lost the race. But since 1999, as each Tour has passed successfully, my experience has grown accordingly, not to mention my stubbornness! As a result, I didn't panic once during the entire race, something I might not have been able to do in 1999 or 2000, for example. But even if it took every ounce of my energy and strength to finally deliver the body blow on my rivals Ullrich, Vinokourov, and Mayo, I fervently believe it has made me an even stronger, more formidable opponent for the years to come.

◀ Liège-Bastogne-Liège was a target for me in the spring, but I made the mistake of going too early and blew up on the final climb. I still want to win this Classic one day.

▲ The Dauphiné-Libéré is the race when Willy Balmat, our traveling Swiss chef, gets into his stride with a huge portfolio of meals to fuel our starving bodies. Willy has been with me since Motorola days. He even comes to my house and cooks when we have private parties!

◄ After Liège, it's time to test the Tour equipment. Mechanic Juan Lujan helps me adjust a seat post during a stage reconnaissance before the Dauphiné-Libéré.

▲ After losing the Dauphiné prologue time trial to Iban Mayo, I wanted to produce a monster ride 3 days later to send a warning to my Tour rivals. On a narrow, twisty, and rolling course, I produced what I think is one of my finest-ever time trials, beating Mayo by a considerable margin and moving comfortably into the race lead. Bike choice had been an important factor here. We opted for a fully aerodynamic frame with tri-bars, despite the slick, tar-melted roads, and the "un-fast" nature of the course.

▶ The stage ended in Saint Heand, hometown of the deceased Andrei Kivilev. His widow and child came on to the podium with me. It was awful to think Kivilev had died just over 3 months ago. He would normally have been a competitor in this very race and no doubt challenging me for the overall victory.

◄◄ **PREVIOUS SPREAD**

Le Train Bleu—once again, we were well in control on stage four to Morzine.
It was so hot that day, there was talk in the peloton of removing our hard-shell helmets,
which is against the rules—but I reasoned with the ringleaders that that would be an insult
to the family of Kivilev who had probably died because he was not wearing a helmet.

▲ My fall didn't stop Mayo from attacking me a few hours later, but I had little trouble staying with him into Chambery. Next day, however, he opened a gap on the Col du Galibier and left me isolated for a while. I am riding a controlled chase and will get back before the finish in Briancon. But I knew I was stiffening up badly, and my back was really giving me trouble.

▲ Another attack on the final climb of the final stage saw Mayo and I dueling for the third time in the Dauphiné. I kept with him without great difficulty and was about to become the winner of the Dauphiné for the second consecutive year.

▲ Mayo and I exchange a handshake on the final podium.

◄ Ouch. I crashed on the rapid descent from Les Gets and needed my wounds cleaned quickly by race doctor Gerard Porte. I wasn't badly hurt, and my team got me back to the peloton quickly. I knew I'd be aching for days to come, maybe weeks, for I'd fallen at about 80 kilometers per hour.

▲ Seventh place in the Parisien prologue was my worst placing in years. It was purely a psychological blow, but an important one for my great rival, Jan Ullrich, who placed fourth.

◀ At long, long last, U.S. Postal won the team time trial in the 2003 Tour, coming back from a 10-second deficit to overtake ONCE by another 30 seconds. It was wonderful for us, as we had taken the first eight places overall and put Victor Hugo Peña, the first-ever Colombian to lead the Tour, into the Yellow Jersey!

▲ The camera doesn't lie. As pleased as I was, I didn't feel at my best in the time trial, but I knew there was still a long way to go.

◀ Iban Mayo, my now-habitual adversary, has attacked at Alpe d'Huez and it is left to me and Heras to do all the chasing;
I was feeling vulnerable and could have had a worse day but only Mayo and Vinokourov gained time on me. Ullrich had lost
1'32", a significant loss that proved to be pivotal once the final classification was calculated 2 weeks from now.

▲ In yellow, but far from happy. I'd discovered my rear brake was rubbing against the wheel all day,
and though I adjusted the brake after the Galibier descent, it had drained me of a lot of strength;
a pity really, as I'd hoped to repeat my stage-winning attack of 2001.

◄◄ **PREVIOUS SPREAD**
No time to admire the scenery this time—we are approaching
the summit of the Col du Lautaret on stage nine to Gap, trying hard
to keep the race together until the final hills of the day.

▲ Beloki's bad crash on stage nine was a big blow to the Tour.
I'd missed it by escaping into a field in a much-publicized drama.
It took away a rival who seemed in the best form of his career.
It could so easily have been me on the ground, and I took
no personal satisfaction at Beloki's misfortune.

► "Are you still there Lance?" is what Ullrich and Zubeldia seem
to be asking on the final climb of stage thirteen. Well I was there,
and they weren't going to get rid of me! Ullrich attacked right
near to the end, but his measly gain of just 7 seconds
made me realize he wasn't doing that well at all.

▲ Hollywood came to the Tour on stage eleven, when Arnold Schwarzenegger followed the stage in one of his Terminator 3 vehicles, which were part of the Tour caravan. He also presented me with the day's Yellow Jersey in Toulouse. It was a change from the pretty Credit Lyonnais girls.

▲ Ullrich attacked on the Col du Tourmalet, and I let him stay in front to fool himself about how strong he thought he was. But I easily caught him before the summit and before the final climb.

▲ Then disaster strikes. I got too close to the spectators and caught a bag in my brake lever. Down I go.

▲ I thought my Tour was over then and there but Mayo had crashed as well.

▲ The crash has stalled the racing, but I was sure Ullrich had accelerated. I got myself back up and started riding again, only to almost fall again after my foot came out of the pedals.

▲ Incredibly, I have got going again—and react to Mayo's premature attack, made while I was still behind everyone. The anger and adrenalin have given me the boost I needed, and now it is me who has attacked. I've dropped Ullrich and am about to do the same to Mayo.

▲ Alone now with 6 kilometers to go, I charge away like a crazy animal. Johan tells me I have gained 20 seconds already. I go faster, as fast as I possibly can go. I used to tell people I always train harder than I ever race. But this was the first time in my career that I had to race harder than I have ever trained.

▶ By the finish, I'm completely shattered and staring up at the clock to see my time. I hoped it was enough to win this damned Tour! It looks good—a gain of 40 seconds over Mayo and Ullrich, and an overall lead of around 1 minute.

▶▶ I can't contain myself as I spot George Hincapie crossing the line many minutes later. The REAL Lance Armstrong has just stood up!

▶ The final showdown with Ullrich came on stage nineteen—
a 49-kilometer time trial from Pornic to Nantes. It was awful weather—
gale-force winds and torrential rain all the way. I held Ullrich to just
a few seconds at the halfway mark, by which time I knew I'd done
enough to win the Tour. Ullrich then fell, at which point I began
to take it even easier and cruised into Nantes a very happy man.

This was one glass of champagne I felt I deserved! But as always, the Tour gives out the cheap stuff, and I'd rather have had a cold beer instead. We'd been given a new team kit for the final day, a redesign of the original U.S. Post Office insignia of the 1950s. It made people laugh a bit, as Postal is often seen as being a very serious team.

▲ I'm on the podium with two very worthy opponents—Jan Ullrich and Alexandre Vinokourov. This had been an epic Tour, a spectacular tribute to 100 years of the Tour de France. But I intend to come to the 2004 Tour in much better shape than I was this year. For I know Ullrich will once again be the man to challenge me the most.

▶ Four of the best—only the late Jacques Anquetil is missing here. I felt honored to pose with five-time winners Bernard Hinault, Eddy Merckx, and Miguel Indurain after the official ceremony was over.

◀◀ **PREVIOUS SPREAD**
Get up here GW. We want our photo taken. Please?

EDDY MERCKX
5-TIME WINNER OF THE TOUR DE FRANCE

It was probably inevitable that Lance and I would become great friends. But I never expected that our friendship would evolve into us both being five-time winners of the Tour de France. When I first met Lance in 1992, he had all the promise of many young cyclists of that age, and his talents seemed perfectly tilted to being a great one-day Classics rider, not a Tour contender at all. I first saw him race as a pro at the Zurich Championships in Switzerland that same year, and he amazed me by taking second place! My bicycles were part of his Motorola Team's sponsorship package, and I could already see the commercial benefit of having an American riding to win on one of my bikes. But I soon grew to love this kid from Texas and cared far less about my bike company's image than I did about wanting to see Lance develop into a top rider.

The very next year I was in Oslo, Norway, when he won the World Championships at the age of 21. I'd gone there hoping someone from my own country would win, but I remember embarrassing my colleagues on the Belgian Cycling Team by jumping for joy when I saw Lance cross the finish line in the pouring rain! Of course before then, Lance had become a much talked about cyclist in Belgium, so nobody really minded—well maybe just a little bit! In those days, Lance would often spend time with me in Belgium. Sometimes we'd go for bike rides near my house in Meise and talk about racing the Classics in Belgium. I thought that

◄ Eddy Merckx with his son Axel, in 1995.

was where Lance's future really lay, as he wanted to know everything about racing on cobbled hills and hiding from the wind in Flanders. It was also at that time that Lance really became friends with my son Axel. They'd both go on longer rides that I could no longer even consider. I think Lance would agree that he had the best meals of his life back then, as my wife, Claudine, always made an extra special recipe when she knew Lance was coming to stay.

Axel was on Lance's team in 1996 when the horrible news broke about his cancer. I was one of the first people Lance told about his illness and both of us were crying over the telephone. It was the worst experience I've ever had to deal with. As soon as Lance was over his first operations, I flew out to Austin and took him out for a bike ride. He was in an awful way, incredibly frail, and he wasn't capable of riding for more than about 40 minutes! He still had the stitches in his head from some brain surgery and was petrified he'd fall and do himself more damage. By this time, I realized how much Lance thought of me, and, in turn, I was always on hand to offer help and encouragement in any way I could. But I never imagined he would come back the way he did in 1998, almost winning the World Championships in The Netherlands and taking fourth place in the Vuelta a España. Still, the best of Lance was yet to come.

If the news of his cancer was the worst thing I can remember of our relationship, his first-ever Tour victory in 1999 was the best thing. I'd seen how much weight Lance had lost through cancer.

He'd always been a reasonable climber, at least on the shorter climbs. And now here he was, ripping apart the opposition to win the Tour de France by a mile! I couldn't have been happier for him, and I knew my joy was shared by others closest to him. All of us had suffered emotionally with Lance's illness, and now suddenly we were all standing on top of the world!

The past years have flown by, and Lance has won six Tours. Lance invited me to his post-Tour party in Paris last July. I wanted to be there to celebrate my friend's incredible achievement. I sat with Lance's closest people including Sheryl Crow and Jim Ochowicz. I last won the Tour in 1974, which was exactly 30 years before Lance won his latest Tour, a unique kind of anniversary! We both had cause to celebrate that night! I loved every minute of that evening. I am in no way jealous or angry that he has now surpassed my five Tours total. I was the best in my time and for sure he is the best Tour rider in his generation by a long, long way.

I think Lance can win one more Tour if he can find the same motivation. I saw a little bit of me in Lance in the 2004 Tour. He wanted to win everything like I used to, on the flat, in the time trials, in the mountains. It was great to see him so free of any other considerations, racing as a 21-year-old races. So maybe he is listening to what I've been telling him all these years...to ride like there's no tomorrow and to take everything you can while you can!

CHAPTER TWELVE

2004: RACING INTO HISTORY

★ I'm now a six-time winner of the Tour de France, the first cyclist to ever win six Tours—and consecutive wins at that. In terms of Tour history, I'm ahead of Anquetil, Hinault, Indurain, and my good friend, Eddy Merckx, who was there to greet me in Paris as I'd always hoped he would be. Like most cyclists this side of fifty years of age, Merckx is my hero, and it feels strange to have passed his tally of Tour victories set way back in the 1970s. Of course, I'm no Eddy Merckx—no one will ever be as good as Eddy—

but it is hard not to feel a huge wave of satisfaction at creating history in the Tour. And it was a huge relief after such a disappointing Tour in 2003 to be there this year, fitter and stronger and more determined than ever before, to show what I was capable of.

To be honest, I'd been preparing for this Tour even before last year's had ended—I was that angry at having let myself be so evidently weak in 2003, to be so exposed to other peoples' strengths and attacks, and to so nearly have wasted the opportunity of a lifetime as well. Accordingly, I set out on a tough winter's campaign, riding longer miles and harder miles than ever before, a hardship set partially aside by the fact I was discovering new routes in and around Los Angeles, where I'd spent a large part of the off-season. The hills and canyons around LA are perfect for training—possibly more than around Austin—because they are that much longer and it is that much hotter.

I landed in Europe in early February—earlier than for many years—determined to show everyone exactly what they'd be con-

Spring training in the Alps was a valuable precondition to winning a sixth Tour de France. Here, I'm climbing the Col de la Madeleine with teammates "Chechu" Rubiera, Jose Azevedo, and "Triki" Beltran, but we'll soon be stopped from going any farther because of winter snows.

tending with that summer. Incredibly, I won a time trial stage of the Volta ao Algarve on February 21, a modest stage-race in southern Portugal, where the peloton was made up largely of domestic Portugese riders. I'd beaten some top guys as well, though, so my performance pleased me a lot, even if it was based more on brute strength and willpower as opposed to race finesse. . . . My girlfriend, Sheryl, was in the following team car, and I know her presence pushed me that little bit harder, as it would do so many other times as the season drifted by—I would make sure she would always be behind me on the days that mattered, for she obviously brought me good luck. With that little win behind me, I was on my way and knew the winter's work had given me the foundation I needed for the months to come.

I missed the entire classics season, preferring to train and race in the States and be with my children. But wins followed in the Tour of Georgia—including a downhill sprint-finish!—and I returned to Europe with about 7 weeks to prepare for the Tour. . . . I deliberately hid my form throughout this period, training incessantly in the Alps. When Iban Mayo won the Dauphiné-Libéré, people started talking about how he was my main threat for the Tour. Of course he was a threat, as was Jan Ullrich, Tyler Hamilton, and many others . . . but they didn't know just how determined I was to step into history and lay last year's ghosts to rest for good. Mind you, I was as puzzled by anyone with my ride up Mont Ventoux in the Dauphiné—that day was as bad as any I can recall—but it served to refocus my efforts on getting into even better shape, physically and mentally, for the similar time trial ascent of Alpe d'Huez on July 21, which is where I expected the Tour to be decided.

In fact, history shows that the Alpe d'Huez was not as decisive as I'd thought, and my opponents were nowhere to be seen when it mattered. It had been a frightening first week's racing with crashes each and every day that threatened to ruin the good start I'd made in the prologue and team time trial stages and on the cobbled roads made famous by Paris-Roubaix. But my nerves settled as we headed into the Pyrenees on stage 12, and from then on I felt stronger each passing day, eventually securing the Yellow Jersey at Villard-de-Lans after outsprinting Ullrich, Andreas Kloden, and Ivan Basso. By now we'd lost Hamilton and Mayo to illness or injuries, and I was a good few minutes in front of the two Germans as well—only Basso was a threat, but I was confident in a head-to-head battle of time trials. There was a huge number of American fans in Villard, waving Lance-6 banners at me on the podium, but I knew there were 2 more very tough days to go, starting with the Alpe d'Huez test the very next day.

I rode to my deepest on that 15.5-kilometer stage, using every ounce of energy I could muster, enhanced by almost a week of training up the very same hill in May. Sheryl was in the following car again, but she was as scared as I was by the behavior of a few of the massive crowds camped out along the hill. Some jeered, some booed, some even spat at me; but thankfully the majority cheered me all the way up, and I put another minute into Ullrich, more so into Kloden and Basso. By then I was really enjoying this Tour. I felt I had done enough to win easily into Paris and couldn't wait for the race's toughest stage the next day—to Le Grand Bornand. It was a superb day, and I worked a one-two with teammate Floyd Landis on the final climb, luring Kloden and Ullrich to make the chase before I outsprinted them all into the finish. If someone had told me 6 years ago that I'd be outsprinting all my rivals this way, I'd have laughed at them. But here I was, doing just that—and loving every second of it!

The rest of this Tour is a blur, as I knew I'd won and wanted just to get to Paris and enjoy it. There was the no-small matter of the Besançon time trial to deal with and the precarious dash across Paris and onto the Champs Elysees, but those barriers fell aside as had all the others, and I crossed the finish line a very happy man that day . . . cheered on by an absolutely huge gathering of friends and spectators right around the circuit. This Tour was definitely one of my happiest, just as 1999 had been. It was as if I'd turned back the clock 6 years to that first Tour win, where I savoured every minute of every day I rode in the Yellow Jersey. Here it was different but no less enjoyable, and I knew I had the support of the best team we'd ever selected.

Of course, I don't want it to stop at six Tours, I'm enjoying myself much too much these days and have discovered talents I never knew I had. Whether I race for a seventh Tour or not, I intend to race for a few more years yet, as I feel I still have a lot to achieve.

▶ Johan and I are debating the difficulties of the Col de la Madeleine during our reconnaissance of stage seventeen of the Tour in May.

▶ I won stage four of the Volta ao Algarve in mid-February—but it hurt! In fact, we were trying out a new position for me as well as a new bike.

▲ ▶ The early-season adrenaline continued over to the Tour of Murcia, where I was racing against both Ullrich and Mayo, who I found myself climbing with on stage four, both of us way behind the leaders!

▲ I returned to Europe after the Tour of Georgia and immediately rode the Alpine stages of the Tour. This included snow-blocked summits like the Col du Glandon, which we cleared ourselves before continuing.

▲ My mini-team on these rides also included Richard Kielpinski, my regular soigneur now, who also lived near me in Girona, Spain.

◀ More time trial testing came in the Criterium Internationale, end of March, but I still finished second to Jens Voigt on the TT stage.

► I took it easy throughout the 5-day Roussillon event but targeted the last stage, which ended atop the Mont St Clair—winning by myself after a battle with a young, tough Euskatel rider.

◄◄ **PREVIOUS SPREAD**
The inaugural Tour du Languedoc-Roussillon was on our list of pre-Tour races in 2004. It takes place in a pretty region of southwestern France, sandwiched between the Pyrenees and the Mediterranean, with some great roads to race on.

▲ This year, the Dauphiné was being handled as just a test, but still I scared myself at how much time I lost in the Mont Ventoux time trial—almost 2 minutes to Iban Mayo! It served to remind me how much work there was still to do.

▶ Although he is a rival team manager, Bjarne Riis and I found time to talk the next morning as we rolled away from the start. Bjarne is a highly intelligent person and a good guy. He is someone I used to race against, and his views are always worth listening to.

▲ By stage four, we were right where we wanted to be—winning the TTT for the second year in succession,
establishing ourselves as the dominant force, and putting me into the race lead,
although we had no plans to defend it . . . for now.

◄ The 2004 Tour departs from Liège. I've never seen so many nervous cyclists as in Belgium—for we all knew how dangerous the day's roads would be in the Ardennes,
and rain was promised too. I was extremely happy with my prologue ride the evening before but knew it was just a tiny step to the ultimate goal—a sixth Tour win.

▲ I somehow missed this big crash at the feed station, but teammates Rubiera, Noval, and Beltran were right in the middle of it. Luckily they were not hurt . . . shaken but not stirred!

▲ Thomas Voeckler was now in Yellow, a beneficiary of the day's long escape, but I was confident that we'd eventually overhaul his 9-minute lead . . . and we would not have to work too hard for 4 to 5 days as well.

◀ Most of stage five was spent ploughing into the headwind and pouring rain—tracked all the way by T-Mobile and Phonak. I'm enjoying a chat with Erik Dekker, while letting a promising escape go clear that would eventually ease the pressure off us.

◀◀ **PREVIOUS SPREAD**
We raced down the Loire Valley on stage six, more concerned with avoiding crashes than looking at the Chateaux.
Today's stage to Angers would see a huge pileup near the finish, but I managed to pull up just in time.

▲ It had been a dangerous week so far—I crashed early during stage six but missed the mass pileup that claimed Gilberto Simoni (far right). Jan Ullrich (middle) was the only one of the favorites to avoid the crashes completely.

◀ Even though stage nine was on safer, hillier roads, I still look terrified of the dangers as Ekimov leads me over a railway crossing partway through the stage. I couldn't wait to get to the mountains now!

◀ Ivan Basso became a new rival for me on stage twelve, beating me into La Mongie but making me even more determined for the next few days.

▲ George and Floyd seem to be laughing their way to the finish, but in fact they are extremely tired after working so hard for me. They were great.

▶ It's me now hurting Basso on stage thirteen, on the climb to Plateau de Beille, with a massive audience of Basque fans. They were scarey, no doubt about that—but I had to believe they were sporting enough to show me respect, even though their hero Mayo had been well and truly dropped.

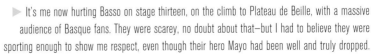

▲ They were also cheering my sprint win over Basso, Kloden, and Ullrich.

▲ Sheryl gave me a victor's kiss; I now knew just how excited she was by the Tour!

▲ This is me acknowledging the fans' cheers in Villard—
but I still felt cautious with the hardest stages still to come.

◄ By now, in the Alps, there were huge numbers of U.S. fans cheering
me and my team on—such as here in Villard-de-Lans on stage sixteen.

◄ This was my supreme effort of the Tour, but I'd ridden Alpe d'Huez so many times in training that I knew just how hard I could go without blowing. It felt great to win by 1 minute!

◄◄ Definitely a day to remember—the time trial to Alpe d'Huez. It was a great feeling to see so many fans cheering me on near the end, but I'd had to race through crowds of rowdy, drunken fans farther down the mountain.

▲ I now felt comfortable at the start of stage seventeen.

▲ Earlier, I'd anticipated the battle with Ullrich
and Kloden on the Col de la Forclaz.

▲ But I owed a lot to Floyd Landis,
who played a major role in my stage victory.

◀ A superb ending to a superb day's racing—
victory at Le Grand Bornand!

◀ The time trial at Besançon may have seemed like a formality, but I still wanted to defend my position. I beat Ullrich by 1 minute again and had now won five stages of this Tour, a record for me. I could relax at last.

▲ As always, the Lone Star was hoisted over the Hotel Crillon the night before we arrived in Paris—I couldn't wait to check in and have my first beer in months!

▲ The traditional champagne toast with Johan had to come first though.

▶ "Okay, six is enough, enough," Jean-Marie Leblanc seems
to be saying to me as we start stage twenty into Paris.

◀ Time for the annual pose in front of the Arc de Triomphe.

▲ A sweet memory for me—showing a number 6 in front of some LAF supporters on the Champs Elysees; these people mean the world to me, I was happy to share the moment with them.

▶ Floyd embarrassed us all with a failed wheelie . . . it's been a long Tour!

GEORGE HINCAPIE
CLOSEST TEAMMATE AND FRIEND

Ask me what I like most about Lance, and I couldn't begin to tell you—for there are too many things. He's the greatest cyclist I've ever known, he's the toughest competitor I've ever met, and he's the most generous person one could want for a friend and teammate. He's also my greatest motivator, and I've loved training and racing alongside him over the years. I first met Lance over 15 years ago, when we were racing together as amateurs in an Olympic trials event in Colorado Springs. Just as now, Lance was a ferocious competitor in those days—and he killed us all! He was determined to go all the way to the top in cycling—that much was obvious. But we got on really well and later found ourselves on the Motorola team when I first turned professional in 1994—that's when our friendship really got going.

Pre-1996, I was pretty much learning the business of pro racing and was a willing student to Lance and Sean Yates—the team's notorious "hardman" and unofficial captain. Thanks partially to their influence, I started winning races in the USA at that time but then continued my education of racing whenever I returned to Europe alongside Lance and Sean. When the news broke of Lance's cancer, I was completely devastated, like most of the guys on the team. I knew something wasn't right with him back in July of '96 when he stopped early on in the Tour de France—that wasn't the Lance I knew. Then in August, I remember looking across at him during the last hour of the Olympic Road Race in Atlanta and

◀ George Hincapie in descending mode at the Vuelta a Murcia, 2003

seeing how much he was suffering—he looked awful, But we just put it down to him having an off day or at worse some sort of virus . . . Boy, how far wrong can anyone have been?

Thankfully, Lance made a full recovery, and by the time he returned to racing in 1998, I was alongside him in nearly all the races he rode. Come '99, we had a new team manager in Johan Bruyneel, and Lance announced he was going to try to win the Tour de France—just like that! But win it he did, and with me right there on some of the mountain climbs. There was a whole new spirit among us now. Gone were the days of uncertainty when we only dreamt of winning the Tour of Flanders or Liège-Bastogne-Liège. With Lance back to full health and with Johan applying his huge amount of experience, we were oozing confidence and had everything to race for. I found myself setting tempo on climbs like the Col du Galibier and Col du Soulor, taking it in turns with Kevin Livingston and Tyler Hamilton to protect Lance for as long as we could. And Lance repayed our work by attacking to win into Sestriere and by killing everyone else in the time trials. It was just fantastic! But I didn't dare believe we'd make it to Paris until I finally saw the Arc de Triomphe on that last stage—we may have looked good, but it had been touch and go the whole way.

Now Lance has won six Tours, and I am proud of the fact I have been there with him all along. There have been ups and downs, of course, most especially in the 2003 Tour, where Lance just wasn't his old self. It took loads of late-night chats to make him be-

lieve he still had it in him to win, despite the fact that Ullrich was breathing right down his neck. My favorite memory was arriving into Luz-Ardiden in the middle of the clouds to see Lance on the podium after he'd won the stage—instinctively we both pointed at each other. It was a very rare, intimate moment for both of us, but especially for me, for I knew that Lance would now win his fifth Tour.

We had no such problems in 2004, but there was still an awful lot of stress in that first week before we could get Lance down to the mountains. The TTT was the worst part of it; there was so much stress before the start with the rain, and then during race we knew we were down on some of the other teams. The last 10-K were awesome when we knew we had it won and we just had to arrive safely . . . a great memory! I was proud to ride along the Champs Elysees with Lance this summer, for I was the only rider on the team who'd been there for all six Tours.

Away from bike races, Lance is an extremely busy man, with obligations to so many people, I am surprised he still has the time to socialize. But he does and shows equal generosity off the bike as well as on it. In October 2001, he sent his private jet to pick me and a few friends up from Las Vegas so that we could be at a party he was holding in Austin. Another time he got me and a friend an invite to the *Sports Illustrated* Sportsman of the Year awards—it was great mixing with so many elite and famous sportsmen. I owe Lance a lot, I sometimes think, but he often tells me how much he owes me—it's not something I take lightly, this respect.

ABOUT THE PHOTOGRAPHER

Twenty-five years later, a career that started with a shot of Merckx rolls on.

Armed with a Pentax Spotmatic camera and a single 200 mm lens, 21-year-old Graham Watson set off from his home in London to capture a few frames of the final day of the 1977 Tour de France. If all went well, Watson would have a bit of adventure in Paris and shoot the finish of the world's greatest race. Watson's first day photographing the Tour happened to be the final day that the legendary Eddy Merckx would ride in the race that he won five times. Whether it was his experience photographing British aristocracy or the sheer luck of a beginner is unclear, but Watson captured an astonishing image of Merckx grinding out the final rain-soaked miles of his storied Tour career. He would sell it to British media mainstay *Cycling Weekly,* and it would be his first cycling photo ever published.

Merckx's grimace through his viewfinder, the grand spectacle of the Tour, and the adventure of simply being out on the road was all Watson needed. This was something he wanted to do for a long time. The following year Watson increased his forays; photographing local races in England, a few Spring Classics in Belgium and a longer stint at the Tour. By the mid-1980s, he was away more than he was home, shooting any race he could find, including the 3-week-long Tours of France, Spain, and Italy.

In the intervening 20 odd years, Graham Watson has captured nearly every important moment in cycling. Watson's history is cycling history: Lemond and Hinault on the Alpe d'Huez, Sean Kelly on the cobbles in Paris–Roubaix, Stephen Roche's World Championship in Austria, Lemond's staggering comeback in the 1989 Tour de France, Indurain's ascension in 1991, Ullrich's surprise Tour victory in 1997, and Armstrong's domination of the race from 1999 through the present. So ubiquitous is his lens, that, if Watson didn't capture it, it likely didn't happen.

With such an astounding catalog of images, Graham could be slowing down, shooting the Tour and not much else. Yet, he still has the eye and enthusiasm of that 21-year-old that shot Merckx's final Tour romp. Like that kid, he is deeply in the thrall of the sport that graces his viewfinder, using his love of both the two-wheeled life and photography as an excuse and invitation to see the world.

—MARK RIEDY

▲ Watson's first recorded image of Lance Armstrong at the 1990 Japanese World Championships.

◄◄ Watson at "work" in the 2001 Tour of Switzerland, with driver Jacky Koch.

◄ Watson shooting frames of Lance's legendary attack on the climb of Luz-Ardiden
in the 2003 Tour de France, thanks to the driving skills of Ismael Borges (front left).

LANCE ARMSTRONG CAREER HIGHLIGHTS

DATE	EVENT NAME	LOCATION	RESULT	DISTANCE	TIME
2004					
02.18.04 to 02.22.04	Tour of Algarve	Spain	5th overall; 1 stage win (stage 4)	709.5 km	19:14:04
4.20.04 to 4.25.04	Tour de Georgia	USA	1st overall; 2 stage wins (stage 3, 4)	1051 km	25:39:20
05.19.04 to 05.23.04	Tour du Languedoc-Roussillon	France	6th overall; 1 stage win (stage 5)	881 km	21:38:53
07.03.04 to 07.25.04	Tour de France	France	1st overall; 6 stage wins (stage 4, 13, 15, 16, 17, 19)	3391 km	83:36:02
2003					
06.08.03 to 06.15.03	Criterium du Dauphiné-Libéré	France	1st; 1 stage win (stage 3)	1187 km	29:31:53
07.05.03 to 07.27.03	Tour de France	France	1st; 2 stage wins (stages 4 and 15)	3427 km	83:41:12
2002					
04.28.02	Amstel Gold Race	Holland	4th	254 km	6:49:17
04.30.02 to 04.31.02	Criterium International	France	2nd	299 km	7:33:04
05.22.02 to 05.26.02	Grand Prix du Midi-Libre	France	1st overall	788 km	19:22:36
06.09.02 to 06.16.02	Criterium du Dauphiné-Libéré	France	1st overall; 1 stage win (stage 6)	1100 km	28:38:50
07.06.02 to 07.28.02	Tour de France	France	1st overall; 4 stage wins (prologue, stage 11, 12 and 19)	3272 km	82:05:12
07.30.02	Profronde van Stiphout	Holland	1st	100 km	–
08.02.02	Rehder City-Night Criterium	Germany	1st	96 km	1:56:56
08.18.02	Championship of Zurich	Switzerland	3rd	236 km	5:58
2001					
04.28.01	Amstel Gold Race	Holland	2nd	254 km	6:39:13
06.19.01 to 06.28.01	Tour of Switzerland	Switzerland	1st overall; 2 stage wins (stages 1 and 8)	1412 km	35:00:06
07.07.01 to 07.29.01	Tour de France	France	1st overall; 3 stage wins (stages 10, 12 and 18)	3455.7 km	86:17:28
2000					
04.25.00	Paris-Camembert	France	2nd	206 km	4:43:23
04.30.00	GP Kanton Aargau/ GP Gippingen	Switzerland	4th	196 km	4:54:10
06.03.00	Classique des Alpes	France	3rd	197 km	5:23:15
06.04.00 to 06.11.00	Criterium du Dauphiné-Libéré	France	3rd overall	1163 km	30:22:43
07.01.00 to 07.23.00	Tour de France	France	1st overall, 2 stage wins (stages 6 and 19)	3630 km	92:33:08
08.27.00	Grand Prix Eddy Merckx TT	Belgium	1st	63.5 km	1:16:18
09.16.00	Grand Prix des Nations	France	1st	75 km	1:31:05
09.27.00	Olympic Games	Australia	13th	239 km	5:30:37
09.30.00	Olympic Games	Australia	3rd	46.8 km	58:14:00
1999					
04.10.99	Circuit de la Sarthe	France	1st stage 4 time trial	16.8 km	20:14
04.24.99	Amstel Gold Race	Holland	2nd	253 km	6:37:23
06.06.99	Criterium du Dauphiné-Libéré	France	1st prologue time trial	6.8 km	9:10
06.22.99	Route du Sud	France	1st stage 4	106 km	3:28:07
07.03.99 to 07.25.99	Tour de France	France	1st overall, 4 stage wins (prologue, stages 8, 9 and 19)	3680 km	91:32:16
07.26.99	Boxmeer Criterium	Holland	1st	100 km	–
1998					
05.22.98	Sprint 56K Criterium/ Ride for the Roses Criterium	USA	1st	56 km	1:03:29
06.11.98 to 06.14.98	Tour of Luxembourg	Luxembourg	1st overall; 1 stage win (stage 1)	726 km	17:14:29

DATE	EVENT NAME	LOCATION	RESULT	DISTANCE	TIME
1998 (continued)					
06.26.98 to 07.02.98	Rheinland Pfalz Rundfahrt	Germany	1st overall	1253 km	31:16:01
07.15.98 to 07.19.98	Cascade Classic	USA	1st overall	379 miles +2 crits	–
08.25.98 to 08.29.98	Tour of Holland	Holland	4th place	897 km	21:08:17
09.05.98 to 09.27.98	Tour of Spain	Spain	4th place	3747 km	93:46:26
10.08.98	World Time Trial Championship	Holland	4th	43.5 km	55:28:00
10.11.98	World Road Race Championship	Holland	4th	258 km	6:02:38
1996					
04.17.96	Fleche Wallone	Belgium	1st	205 km	4:40:00
04.21.96	Liège-Bastogne-Liège	Belgium	2nd	263 km	6:58:02
05.01.96 to 05.12.96	Tour DuPont	USA	1st overall; 5 stage wins (stage 2, 3b, 5, 6 and 12)		48:20:05
07.31.96	Olympic Games Road Race	USA	12th	222 km	4:54:24
08.03.96	Olympic Games Time Trial	USA	6th	52 km	1:06:28
1995					
03.05.95 to 03.12.95	Paris-Nice	France	1st stage 5	176 km	4:03:20
04.25.95 to 05.07.95	Tour DuPont	USA	1st overall; 3 stage victories (stage 4, 5 and 9)	1131 miles	46:31:16
04.23.95 to 04.28.95	Kmart Classic	USA	1st overall; 1 stage victory (stage 4)	474 miles	21:12:57
05.21.95	Thrift Drug Classic	USA	2nd	108 miles	4:27:09
07.01.95 to 07.23.95	Tour de France	France	1st (stage 18)	166.5 miles	3:47:53
08.15.95	Clasica San Sebastian	Spain	1st	230 km	5:31:17
1994					
4.94	Liège-Bastogne-Liège	Belgium	2nd	268.5 km	7:17:37
5.94	Thrift Drug Classic	USA	1st	113 miles	4:42:25
05.04.94 to 05.15.94	Tour DuPont	USA	2nd	1050 miles	47:15:53
1993					
5.93	First Union Grand Prix	USA	1st	1118 miles	4:14:27
05.23.93	Thrift Drug Classic	USA	1st	118 miles	4:47:34
05.93	Kmart Classic	USA	1st overall; 2 stage wins	493.5 miles	19:59:26
05.93	Tour DuPont	USA	2nd overall	1768.8 km	46:44:26
06.06.93	Corestates US Pro Championship	USA	1st	156 miles	6:19:39
6.93	US Nat'l Road Race Championship	USA	1st	156 miles	6:19:38
8.93	Leeds Classic	England	5th	231 km	5:42:12
07.12.93	Tour de France	France	1st (stage 8)	184 km	4:22:23
08.30.93	World Road Championship	Norway	1st	160 miles	6:17:10
1992					
5.92	First Union Grand Prix	USA	1st	118 miles	4:25:15
5.92	Thrift Drug Classic	USA	1st	115 miles	4:52:49
06.17.92	US National Road Race Championships	USA	2nd	128 miles	5:12:37
8.92	Tour of Galicia	Spain	111th overall; 1st in one stage	–	6:25:17
8.92	Championship of Zurich	Switzerland	2nd	240 km	6:00:16